A Guide to Happy and Calm Days

Techniques to Manage Big Feelings for Children

Wonder House

(An imprint of Prakash Books)

contact@wonderhousebooks.com

ISBN : 978-93-70897-47-2

Acknowledgements

To our mentors, our deepest gratitude for your guidance and encouragement.

To our families, thank you for showing how beautiful the world of emotion can be.

To Aryana, Swara Ghosh, Meher Soni and Parth Sehgal, thank you for being the age-experts and consultants on this book.

To our publisher, Payal Jaipuria, editor, Nidhi and designer, Ahmad Hilal, thank you in the creation of this book.

To our readers, thank you for picking up this book. In today's fast-paced world, where peace can be hard to come by, we have created a guide that will take you through a journey of self-discovery. By being aware and accountable, we can reshape our emotions and change our narratives, and make this world a little more welcoming.

About the Authors

Dr. Pragati Jalan Sureka is a distinguished psychologist, therapist and educator with over two decades of experience in mental health and emotional wellness. She is the creator of the Emotional Ability Resources (EaR) Model—an innovative framework for emotional intelligence researched, developed and incubated at Harvard. Her work integrates insights learned from programs at Harvard Medical School, University of Cambridge, INSEAD, BALM, CCC and Sangath, reflecting a rare blend of clinical expertise and management acumen.

An alumna of the Indian Institute of Management (IIM) Kolkata, Dr. Sureka's approach combines psychology, education and leadership principles to make emotional health accessible and actionable. She has authored eleven books on emotional well-being and spoken at global platforms, such as the World Economic Forum, TEDx and the Frankfurt Book Fair.

Dr. Sureka's mission is to redefine emotional intelligence as a core life skill—one that can be nurtured from childhood to leadership. Through her writing, teaching and training, she continues to inspire individuals, educators and organizations to embrace emotions as pathways to growth, resilience and empathy.

About the Authors

Devaleena Ghosh is a Clinical Psychologist, Life Coach and Workshop Facilitator with over two decades of experience in mental health and personal development. Her expertise lies in helping women recover from Narcissistic Abuse and Approval Addiction (Codependency), guiding them to reclaim self-worth, establish healthy boundaries and live emotionally empowered lives. Having worked with thousands of individuals, Ghosh integrates deep psychological insight with practical, compassionate strategies that foster healing, resilience and authentic self-expression. Her work emphasizes the importance of emotional literacy as a foundation for lifelong well-being, advocating its inclusion in school curricula to help children grow into emotionally balanced adults.

She is the co-author of *Draw The Line*, written with Dr. Pragati Sureka, which explores boundary-setting as a transformative act of self-care. The book blends modern psychological research with ancient Vedic wisdom to help readers cultivate clarity, balance and self-respect—empowering them to create healthier, more fulfilling relationships and lives.

TABLE OF CONTENTS

Section III: Strategies for Anxiety

Section IV: People Around Me

Section V: Understanding Anxiety in Specific Situations

Section 1

Understanding Anxiety

CHAPTER 1

The Sneaky Guest Called Anxiety

Once upon a time, in the bustling little town of Surat, there lived an 8-year-old girl named Riya. She had a bright smile, a love for drawing and a heart full of dreams. But there was something else in her life that was not so bright—she was always worried.

You see, anxiety is like an uninvited guest that sometimes sneaks into our minds and makes us feel worried. It's completely normal to feel anxious from time to time, but when it starts showing up too often, it can feel like a big, dark cloud that won't go away.

So, let's break it down and learn more about anxiety and how it can show up in our lives.

What Is Anxiety?

Anxiety is like having a worry monster that won't leave you alone. It's when your brain gets stuck thinking about things that could go wrong, even when everything seems okay.

Symptoms of Anxiety and Where It Likes to Hang Out:

Anxiety: It's that sneaky little emotion that creeps up when you least expect it. Just like how Riya's tummy hosted a butterfly party when she had a big math test, anxiety has its own unique ways of showing itself.

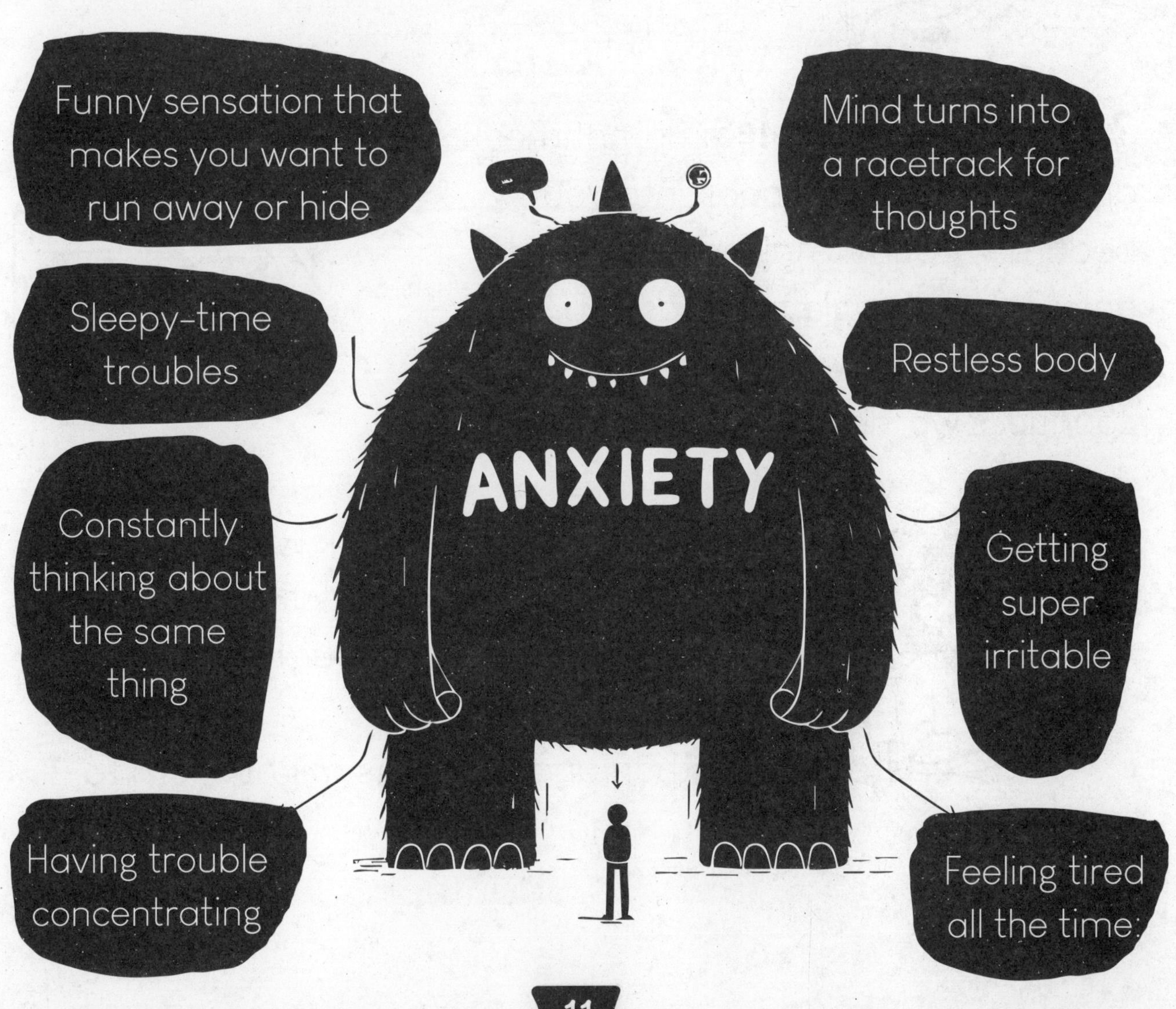

1. Butterflies in the Tummy: Ever had that feeling where a bunch of fluttery butterflies decided to have a party in your tummy? That's anxiety for you. The tummy yearns to join the butterflies on a jungle adventure rather than tackle problems.

2. Racing Thoughts: Anxiety can also turn your mind into a racetrack for thoughts. It's like your brain suddenly transforms into a speedy cheetah, making it nearly impossible to focus on anything else.

3. Bedtime Troubles: Sometimes, anxiety decides to sneak into your bedtime routine, making it feel like an eternal struggle to fall asleep. You toss and turn as your mind spins with countless worries.

4. Restless Body: Anxiety can also turn your body into a restless squirrel with way too much energy. Your hands might fidget, your heart might race like it's in a marathon and your legs might seem to have a mind of their own.

5. Tummy Troubles: Sometimes, anxiety can make your tummy feel like it's tied up in knots. You might feel queasy or need to run to the bathroom more often.

6. Worrying: Anxiety can feel like the worries are taking over the whole brain. You might think about the same thing over and over again, like a broken record that won't stop playing.

7. Avoiding Things: When something makes you nervous, it's natural to want to avoid it. But avoiding things can become a bigger problem.

8. Getting Super Irritable: Ever feel like you're about to erupt like a volcano over something small? That's how it can feel when anxiety starts to bubble up inside you. You might snap at your friends or family for no reason at all.

9. Feeling Tired All the Time: Anxiety can be exhausting! Even if you've had a good night's sleep, you might still feel like you need a nap halfway through the day. That's because your body is using up all its energy worrying about things.

10. Having Trouble Concentrating: When your brain is busy worrying, it can be hard to focus on anything else. You might find it tough to pay attention in class or even while playing your favorite video game.

Remember, everyone's different, so you might not have all these symptoms even if you're feeling anxious.

Now, let's learn a few more things about anxiety. It isn't picky about where it likes to hang out in our bodies. It's like a puzzle, where our feelings and thoughts connect to our physical sensations.

1. Heart and Tummy: Sometimes, anxiety camps out in the heart and tummy. The heart races like it is in a hurry, while the tummy feels like it is hosting a never-ending butterfly extravaganza.

2. Head: Sometimes, you get a headache from overthinking. It's as if a little storm is brewing in your mind, creating dark clouds of anxiety.

3. Muscles: During the peak of anxiety, your shoulders and neck might tense up so much that it can feel like you're carrying an invisible backpack filled with bricks.

4. Breathing: When anxiety knocks, your breath can turn shallow and quick.

Understanding where anxiety hides in your body helps you realize it isn't just a mental battle; it is a full-body experience.

Remember, there might be situations that make you feel extremely worried or afraid. But as you learn to pinpoint those tricky thoughts that trigger fear or fluttering butterflies in your tummy, you'll realize they're often not as daunting as they seem. You have the power to conquer those fears and own your world.

CHAPTER 2

Meeting Anxiety

Have you ever wondered why some of us carry around more worries than others? Let's dive into this fascinating topic and discover why some children might feel a little extra anxious.

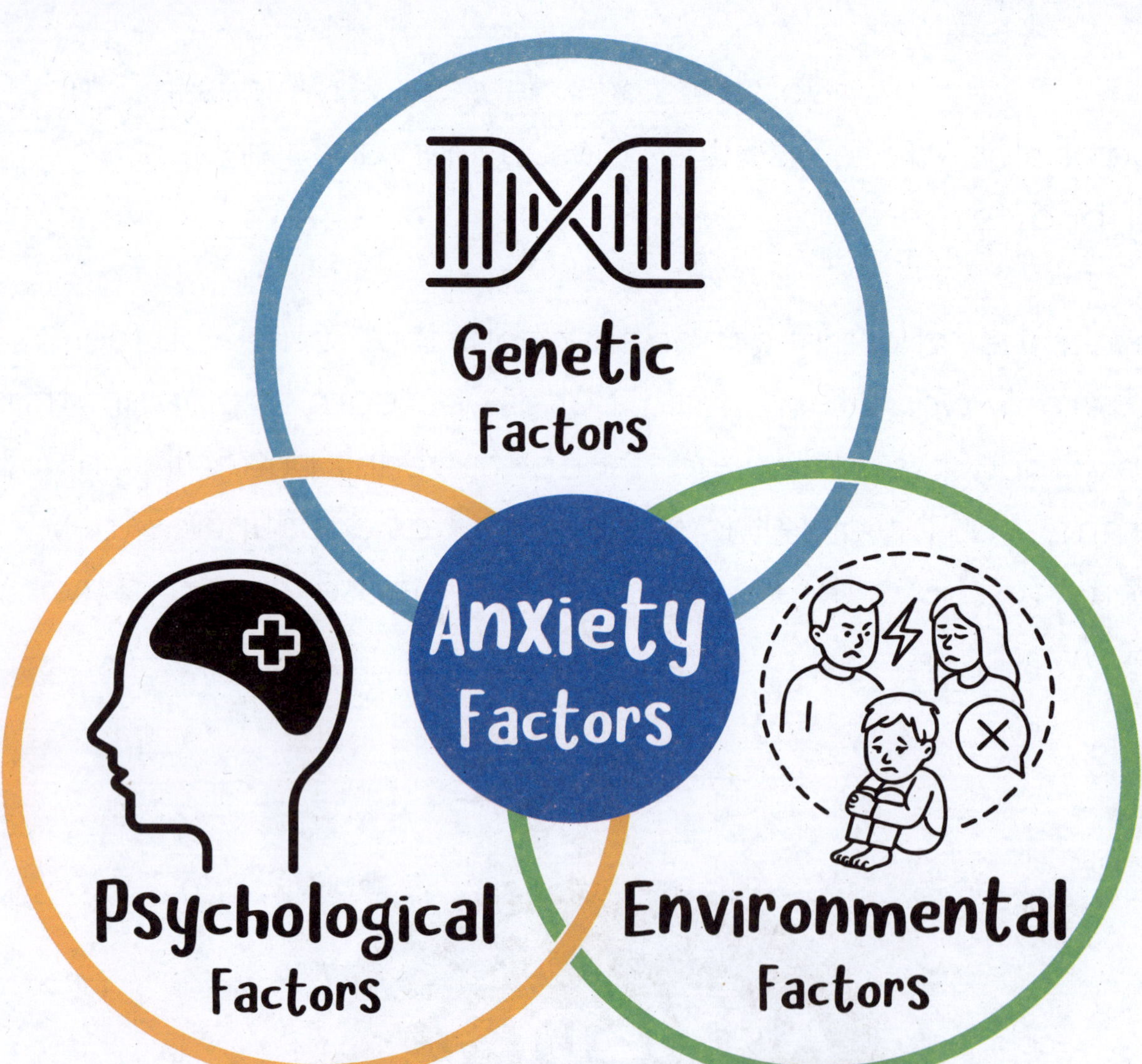

1. Genetic Factors: Imagine your body as a big puzzle, with each piece playing a part in how you feel. For some, their genes can make them more prone to feeling anxious. It's like they've inherited a special worry gene!

2. Psychological Factors: Think of your mind as a busy playground, with lots of thoughts and feelings running around. Some have a temperament that makes them more sensitive to feelings like worry. It's like their worry switch is turned up a little higher.

3. Environmental Factors: Growing up in a home where people worry a lot or experiencing tough times can make us feel more anxious.

So, there you have it! While anxiety might feel like a big, mysterious monster, understanding where it comes from can help us face it with courage.

CHAPTER 3

Different Ages and Anxiety

When you're around 6 months to 3 years old, it's common to feel a bit shaky when you're away from your grown-ups. You might cling to your mom or dad, but by the time you're 2 or 3, you'll start feeling more secure about them going away.

As you grow a bit older, you might find yourself shaking in your boots about specific things. Suddenly, bugs, storms or even the dark start giving you the creeps! These fears usually show up out of the blue and disappear just as fast. So, don't fret too much if you're scared of shadows today—they'll likely be gone tomorrow!

How Anxiety Shows Up at Different Ages:

For Babies (0-2 Years Old): When babies are very little, they rely on their parents or caregivers for everything, like food, cuddles and safety. Sometimes, babies can feel worried when their mom or dad leaves the room, even for a short time. This is called separation anxiety.

For Young Kids (2-6 Years Old):

As kids get a little older, they start to use their imagination more. That's when they might start thinking about things that seem scary but aren't real, like monsters under the bed or ghosts in the dark. They might also feel a little nervous about going to a new place, like school or daycare, without their parent. Over time, they usually start feeling more comfortable in new places, especially when they make new friends and have fun.

For Kids in Elementary School (6-10 Years Old): When kids are in elementary school, they start to care more about real-life things, like doing well in school, making friends and being liked by others. Sometimes, they might worry about making mistakes or not being good enough at something. This is called anxiety. It's okay to feel this way, and there are ways to help them feel better, like taking deep breaths or talking to a trusted adult.

For Teens (12-18 Years Old):

When kids become teenagers, they go through a lot of changes, both in their bodies and their emotions. They might feel stressed about things like schoolwork, fitting in with their friends or what they want to do when they grow up. This can sometimes make them feel anxious.

There might be other times in your life when those jitters creep up on you, like when you're stepping into a new school or staring down a big, scary test. It's all part of growing up.

How Do You Respond?

Circle the way you respond when you are upset or worried about something.

Fight	Flight	Freeze
Yelling or arguing	Running away	Feeling paralyzed or stuck
Hitting or pushing	Avoiding the situation	Withdrawing socially
Becoming aggressive	Hiding	Feeling overwhelmed
Defending aggressively	Seeking a safe place	Feeling scared or panicked

CHAPTER 4

Anxiety and Her Friends

Let's talk about different types of anxiety. Just like there are different kinds of feelings, there are also different kinds of anxiety.

Generalized Anxiety Disorder (GAD): Imagine feeling worried or anxious almost all the time, even when there's no specific reason to be. That's what it's like for someone with Generalized Anxiety Disorder (GAD). They might feel restless, easily tired or have trouble concentrating. Sometimes, their muscles might feel really tense or they might have a hard time sleeping.

Social Anxiety Disorder: Some people get really nervous in social situations. For them, it's more than just feeling shy—it's Social Anxiety Disorder. They might worry a lot about being judged or fear being embarrassed. This can make it hard for them to do everyday things.

Separation Anxiety Disorder:

Separation Anxiety Disorder is when you feel really anxious or upset about being apart from someone you love, like your parents or caregivers. You might worry that something bad will happen to them if you're not with them or feel scared to be away from home.

Specific Phobias: They're intense fears of certain things, like spiders, heights or crowded places. People with phobias go out of their way to avoid these things because they make them feel really anxious. Imagine being so scared of something that you can't even be near it!

Panic Disorder: A person with Panic Disorder feels all their thoughts racing in a negative downward spiral. They think the worst will happen to them. Their heart beats faster, and they feel dizzy and breathless. Everything seems to be collapsing for them, and they are unable to think or act in a reasonable manner.

Each type of anxiety comes with its own set of challenges, but it's important to remember that help and support are available. You're not alone, and there are ways to manage and overcome anxiety, so you can live a happy and fulfilling life.

Feeling a little nervous or scared sometimes is completely normal—it's part of being human! But if those feelings stick around for a long time, like more than two or three months, and start to get in the way of doing things you enjoy, it might be time to talk to someone about it. You've got this!

1. Social Anxiety Disorder

2. Separation Anxiety Disorder

Generalized Anxiety Disorder (GAD)

4. Panic Disorder

3. Specific Phobias

CHAPTER 5

When Do Worries Become Worrisome

Now, let's talk about when the worries start causing a ruckus in your life.

Imagine you're in school and everyone's feeling a bit antsy because of a big test coming up. While some kids are just a bit jittery, others are downright paralyzed with fear. Some might even miss school altogether because those butterflies in their tummy won't settle down. When anxiety gets this intense, you might start feeling like you want to hide away from everything and everyone.

So, let's dive in and figure out when worries become a big deal.

Signs of Anxiety

In Yourself:

1. Mood Swings: Do you feel more irritable, sad or overwhelmed than usual?

2. Sleep Struggles: Are you tossing and turning at night or waking up feeling more tired than usual?

3. Physical Symptoms: Pay attention to any changes in your body, like headaches, stomachaches or muscle tension.

4. Difficulty Concentrating: Are you finding it hard to focus on tasks or remember things?

5. Avoiding Stuff: Notice yourself dodging activities or situations that used to be no big deal?

In Your Friends

1. Changes in Behavior: Keep an eye out for any big shifts in your friend's behavior, like being more withdrawn or agitated than usual.

2. Talks About Worries: If your friend starts opening up about feeling stressed or anxious, it's a good sign they might need some extra support.

3. Physical Signs: Just like with yourself, watch for any physical signs of distress in your friend, like headaches, stomachaches or trouble sleeping.

4. Social Withdrawal: Notice your friend pulling back from social activities or avoiding hanging out with friends? It could be a sign they're feeling overwhelmed.

5. Changes in Routine: Any sudden changes in your friend's routine, like skipping meals or neglecting hobbies they used to enjoy, might be red flags for worry.

It's okay to feel nervous or worried sometimes—that's just part of being human! But when those worries start taking over your life, that's when it's time to act. You've got this!

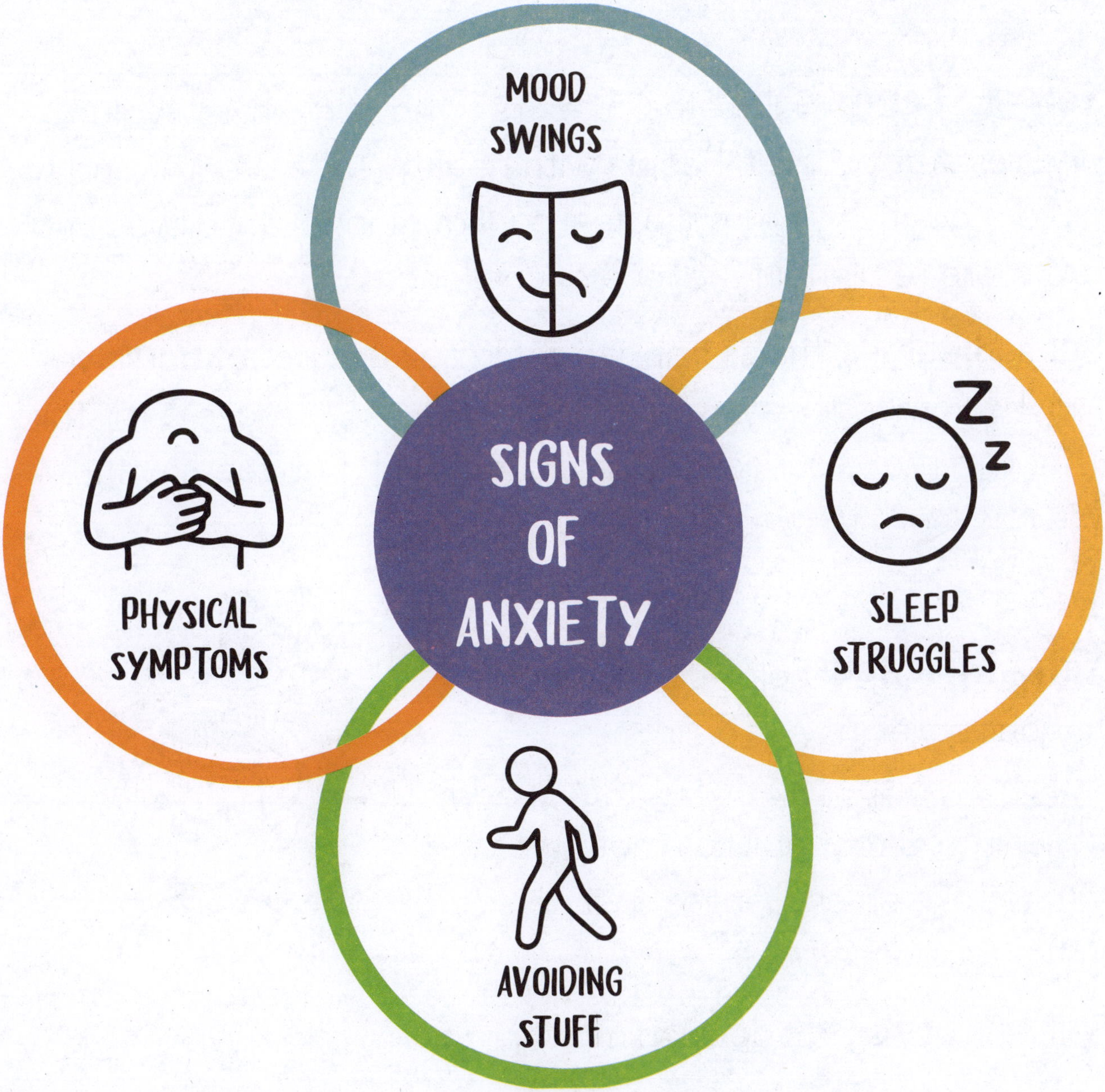

MOOD SWINGS

SIGNS OF ANXIETY

PHYSICAL SYMPTOMS

SLEEP STRUGGLES

AVOIDING STUFF

CHAPTER 6

Impact of Anxiety on Self-Esteem, Self-Efficacy and Confidence

Self-Esteem: Self-esteem refers to how much you value and respect yourself. People with healthy self-esteem tend to have a positive self-image, feel confident in their abilities and are more resilient in the face of challenges.

But sometimes, things happen that make us doubt ourselves. Maybe someone says something mean or we make a mistake. That can make our self-esteem drop a bit. But guess what? We can learn to boost it back up!

Self-Efficacy: Self-efficacy relates to your belief in your ability to accomplish specific tasks or goals. This belief in your capabilities motivates you to take on challenges and persist in the face of setbacks.

Self-efficacy starts developing when you're a kid. Whenever

you learn something new or try something different, your self-efficacy gets stronger. It keeps growing as you go through life, making you better at lots of things.

Confidence: Confidence is closely related to self-esteem and self-efficacy. It's the assurance and self-assuredness you have in your abilities and judgment.

As we become more confident, we don't get upset as easily, and we start believing that we can make good things happen.

Impact of Anxiety

Anxiety can significantly impact self-esteem, self-efficacy and confidence in various ways:

1. Self-Esteem: Anxiety can erode self-esteem by causing negative self-talk and self-doubt. When individuals constantly worry, they may develop a critical inner voice that undermines their self-worth. For example, a child with anxiety might think, "I'm always so anxious; I must be weak," leading to lowered self-esteem.

Emma was a bright and creative 11-year-old who loved painting and playing with her friends. There was a tiny voice inside her head that kept saying, "You're not good enough." This voice made her worry about school and whether her friends truly liked her.

Slowly, her self-esteem started slipping away like sand through her fingers.

One sunny day, Emma decided she didn't want to feel this way anymore. She talked to her parents, who listened closely to her worries. They told her that she was wonderful just as she was and that her uniqueness was what made her special.

With her family's support, Emma started painting again and inviting her friends over to play. She realized that she was good at many things and that she was loved for being herself. Over time, the voice of anxiety grew quieter, and Emma's self-esteem blossomed like a beautiful flower.

2. Self-Efficacy: Anxiety often makes people doubt their abilities. The constant fear of making mistakes or failing can diminish one's belief in their capacity to handle challenges. This reduced self-efficacy can result in avoidance behaviors, preventing individuals from trying new things or pushing their boundaries.

Manish was a smart kid, but he had a problem—his new school project. The more he thought about it, the more he worried that he might make mistakes or mess it up. Manish's worries made him doubt his abilities, and he felt like he couldn't do anything right. One day, Manish decided to talk to his favorite teacher, Mrs. Raina, about his worries. She told him that making mistakes was a part of learning and that even grown-ups made them.

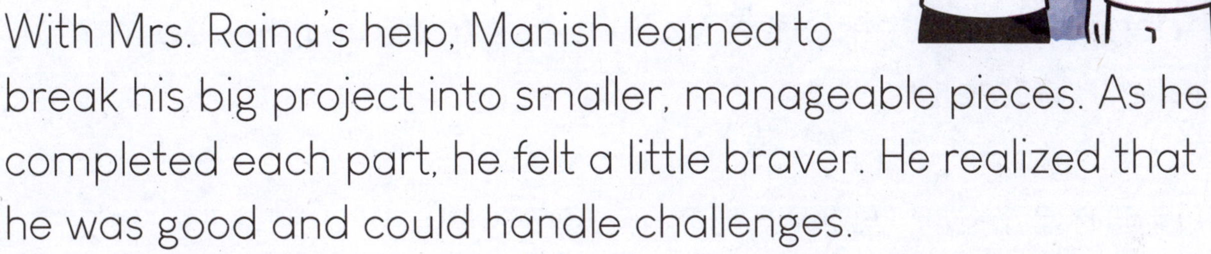

With Mrs. Raina's help, Manish learned to break his big project into smaller, manageable pieces. As he completed each part, he felt a little braver. He realized that he was good and could handle challenges.

3. Confidence: Anxiety can lead to self-doubt and second-guessing, diminishing one's confidence in decision-making and problem-solving. Anxious individuals may become hesitant to assert themselves or express their opinions, fearing judgment or criticism.

In a friendly neighborhood, there lived a 9-year-old girl named Sarah. She was known for her kindness and creativity, but she had a little secret—she sometimes felt unsure about speaking up.

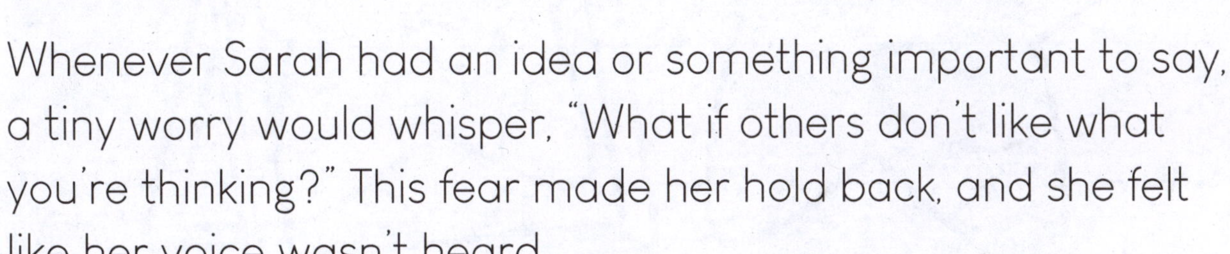

Whenever Sarah had an idea or something important to say, a tiny worry would whisper, "What if others don't like what you're thinking?" This fear made her hold back, and she felt like her voice wasn't heard.

One sunny day, Sarah decided that it was time to face her

worries head-on. She joined a special class that helped kids like her become more confident. With the help of her understanding teacher and her loving family, she practiced speaking up and sharing her thoughts.

As the days passed, Sarah noticed something wonderful happening. Her confidence started to grow, and she began to believe in herself more.

While anxiety can diminish these concepts, with the right support and strategies, individuals can rebuild and strengthen their belief in themselves, ultimately reclaiming their sense of self-worth and empowerment.

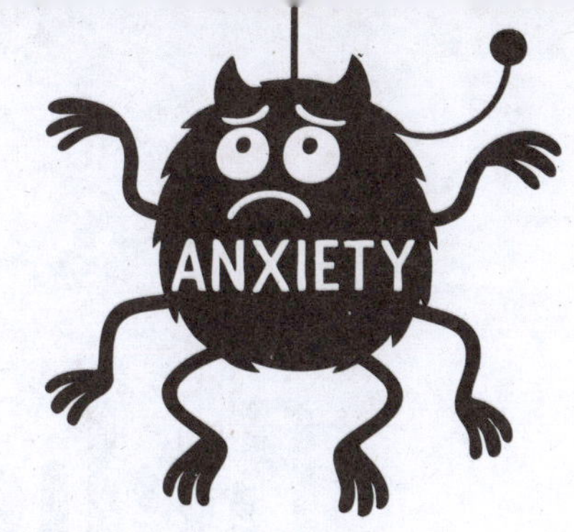

ANXIETY

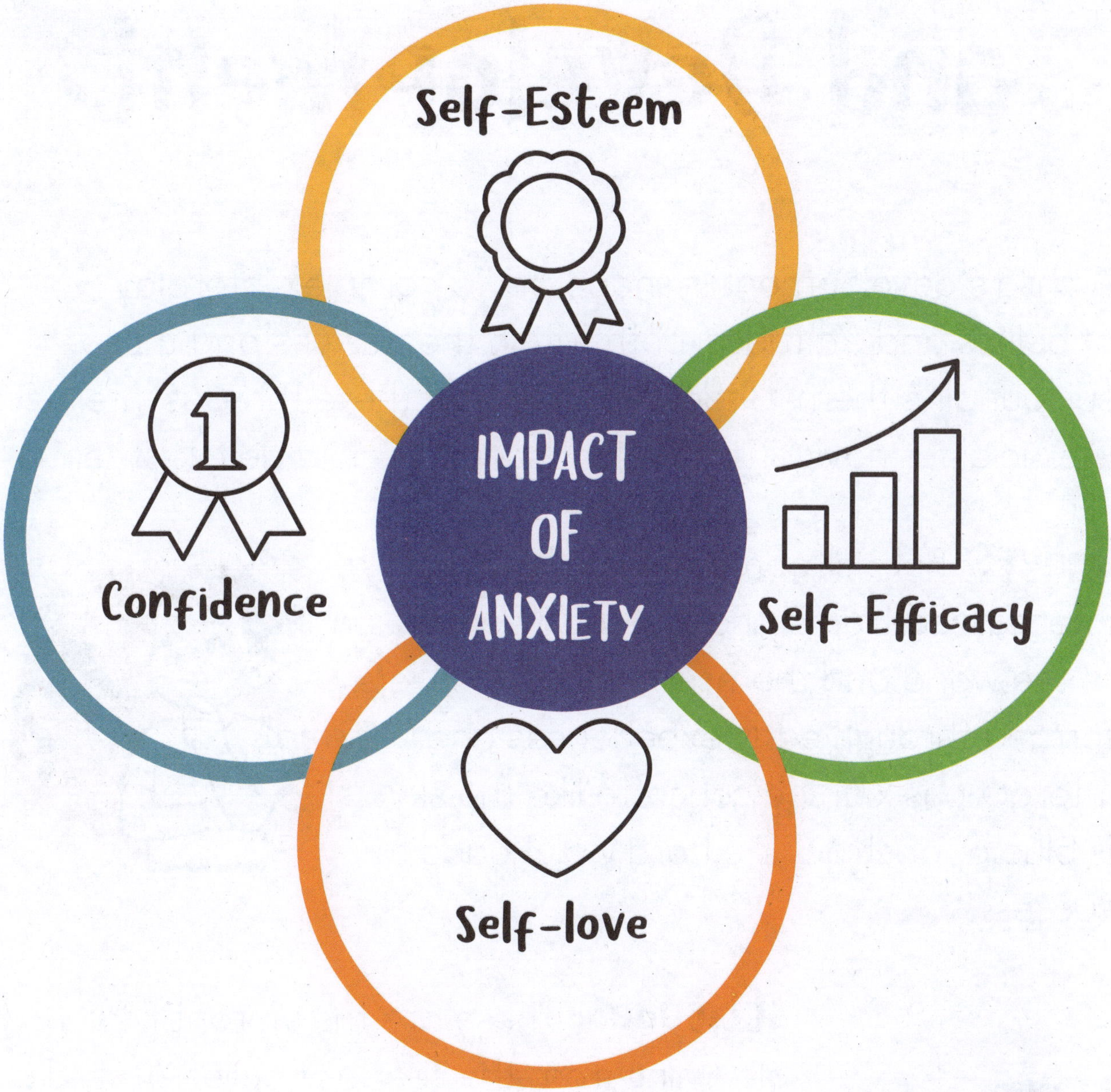
Self-Esteem
Confidence
IMPACT OF ANXIETY
Self-Efficacy
Self-love

CHAPTER 7

Beliefs, Attitudes and Development

A child's development is shaped by a complex interplay of beliefs and attitudes, both within themselves and those surrounding them. Understanding how these threads interact is crucial for navigating the landscape of child development.

Beliefs: Beliefs represent a child's internalized truths, shaping their perception of the world and themselves. These beliefs, formed through early experiences and interactions, can be concrete like the sky is blue or abstract like hard work leads to success.

Attitudes: These are the vibrant flowers blooming from the seeds of belief. Attitudes represent a child's emotional response and evaluation of situations and people. A child who believes in kindness might develop a warm and helpful attitude toward others, while a child who believes in personal strength might have a determined attitude toward challenges.

However, the relationship between beliefs and attitudes is dynamic and reciprocal. Positive attitudes can strengthen positive beliefs, creating a virtuous cycle.

Faulty Beliefs: When Perceptions Get Misaligned

Faulty beliefs are ideas or assumptions we hold about ourselves, the world and others that are not accurate or helpful. They can be formed through various experiences, including childhood upbringing, cultural influences or even personal biases. While not inherently harmful, faulty beliefs can become problematic when they lead to negative thoughts, emotions and behaviors.

Instead of presenting a clear picture, they distort reality, impacting how we interpret situations and interact with others.

Inaccurate: They don't reflect reality accurately, leading to misinterpretations and misunderstandings.

Unhelpful: They hinder our ability to cope with challenges, achieve goals and build healthy relationships.

Rigid: They resist change and adaptation, making it difficult to learn from new experiences and adjust to different situations.

Self-Defeating: They fuel negative self-talk and limit our potential by reinforcing limiting beliefs about ourselves.

Examples:

"I'm not good enough." This can lead to low self-esteem, perfectionism and anxiety.

"People are always judging me." This can lead to social anxiety and difficulty trusting others.

"The world is a dangerous place." This can lead to fear, isolation and difficulty in taking risks.

"I always have to be in control." This can lead to stress, difficulty trusting others and difficulty delegating tasks.

It's important to remember that everyone has faulty beliefs to some degree. The key is to recognize them, understand their impact and work toward replacing them with more accurate and helpful beliefs. This can be done through self-reflection, cognitive restructuring techniques, therapy and seeking support from loved ones.

By acknowledging and shifting our faulty beliefs, we can open ourselves to a more positive and fulfilling experience of life.

Write a letter to your parents and explain how you feel, along with what you have learned till now from this book.

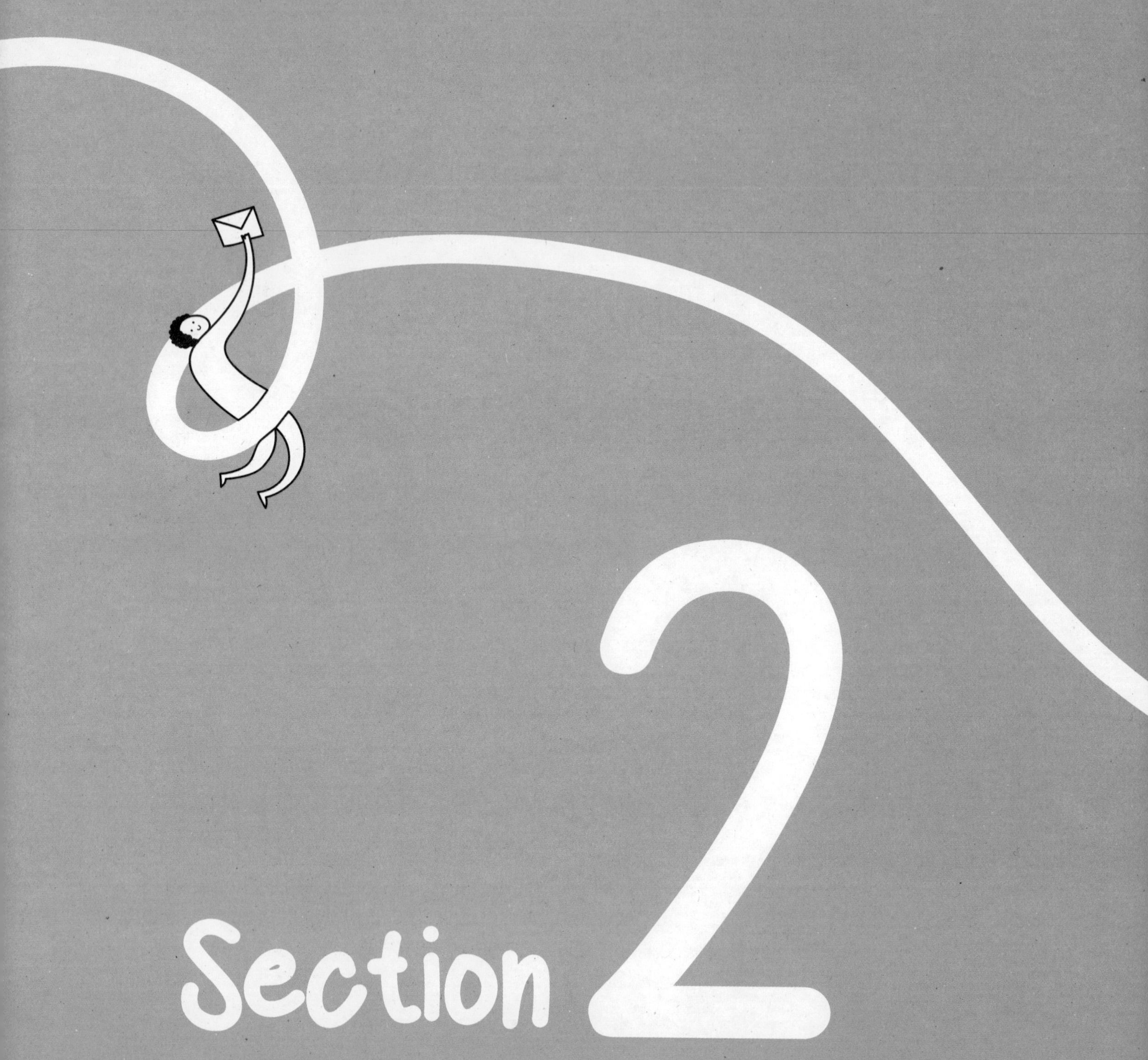

Section 2

Communicating About Anxiety

CHAPTER 1

Communication and Its Impact

What Is Effective Communication?

Imagine a super-secret club!

Have you ever whispered a secret to your best friend or played a game of charades where you acted things out without talking? That's communication! But how does it work?

The Process of Communication

Communication is a two-way street. There's a sender, who sends a message, and a receiver, who gets it. But it's not just about talking! We need to use a shared language and understand each other's feelings to communicate effectively.

1. Sending a Message: Imagine sending a letter to a friend. You write your message, put it in an envelope and send it through the mail.

2. Receiving the Message: Your friend receives the letter and reads it. But here's the cool part: they don't just read the words. They understand the meaning based on their knowledge, feelings and experiences.

3. Giving Feedback: Your friend writes back to you, sharing their thoughts and feelings. This is called feedback, and it helps keep the conversation going!

Communication helps us learn and grow.

Level Up with Effective Communication!

Imagine being the ultimate communicator, sending messages so clear that everyone understands exactly what you mean.

Being an effective communicator isn't just about talking and listening. It's like being a master code breaker, understanding not just the words, but also the feelings and intentions behind them.

Here Are Some Super Skills to Level Up Your Communication Game:

1. Be a Mind Reader (Well, Almost!)

Pay attention to your friend's body language and tone of voice. Are they smiling and nodding? Or frowning and crossing their arms? These clues can help you understand their feelings and talk to them clearly.

2. Choose the Right Channel

Is it a whisper for a secret, a loud shout for excitement or a written note for something special? Choosing the right way to deliver your message helps make sure it gets heard loud and clear!

3. Speak in Code, but the Good Kind

Use words and phrases that your friend understands. Avoid confusing jargon or slang.

4. Listen Like a Ninja

Don't just wait for your turn to talk! Really listen to what your friend is saying, ask questions and show you're interested.

5. Check for Understanding

After you share your message, ask your friend if they understood it. If they didn't, try saying it in a different way.

By using these super skills, you can become a master communicator, building stronger friendships.

CHAPTER 2

Importance of Effective Communication

A Tale of Communication Catastrophe

Deep within the lush Amazon rainforest, two explorers, Anya and Kai, stumbled upon a hidden temple. Thrilled by the prospect of ancient secrets, they ventured inside, only to be met with a series of cryptic murals and indecipherable inscriptions. Their initial excitement soon morphed into frustration, as miscommunication turned their exploration into a comedic disaster.

Anya, a meticulous planner, deciphered the symbols based on logical deductions. Kai, on the other hand, interpreted the murals through his artistic lens, seeing them as metaphors and riddles. They argued over the meaning of a jaguar symbol. Anya insisted it represented a hidden trap,

while Kai saw it as a symbol of courage.

Just as they were about to give up, they encountered a wise old shaman. He explained that the key to unlocking the temple's secrets lay not in deciphering symbols, but in understanding each other. He guided them through exercises that built trust and encouraged them to see the world from each other's perspectives.

Anya learned to simplify her language and appreciate Kai's intuitive insights. Kai, in turn, honed his communication skills and learned to express his creative ideas more clearly. Anya's logic combined with Kai's creativity led them to crack the code, revealing the temple's hidden treasure.

Why Is Effective Communication Important?

Imagine you're in the middle of an intense game, and you need to pass the ball to your teammate. If you don't communicate clearly, they might not understand your signal, and the game could go off track. Effective communication helps us avoid misunderstandings and keeps things running smoothly in our friendships, schoolwork and family life.

1. Building Strong Relationships: When we communicate clearly and openly, we build trust and understanding, which strengthens our bonds with others.

2. Resolving Conflicts: When we're able to express our thoughts and feelings calmly and listen to others with empathy, we can find solutions that work for everyone involved.

3. Achieving Goals: When we clearly communicate our ideas, delegate tasks and provide feedback, we can accomplish our goals more efficiently.

4. Expressing Ourselves: Whether we're speaking up in class, sharing a story with friends or expressing our creativity through art or music, communication is how we make our voices heard.

5. Advancing in Life: Whether we're applying for a job, giving a presentation or advocating for a cause we believe in, strong communication skills can open doors and create opportunities.

By honing our communication skills, we can build stronger relationships, resolve conflicts peacefully, achieve our goals, express ourselves confidently and create a brighter future for ourselves and others.

The more you practice your communication skills, the more you'll unlock these amazing benefits in your own life. The next time you find yourself lost in a jungle of misunderstandings, remember Anya and Kai's journey. With a little effort and open communication, you too can transform confusion into collaboration and unlock the hidden treasures.

CHAPTER 3

Exploring the Family Communication Patterns Theory

Let us now understand how families communicate and why it matters so much. Imagine your family as a team where each person plays a special role. The **Family Communication Patterns Theory (FCPT)** helps us understand how families work together to create a shared understanding of each other, making them even stronger!

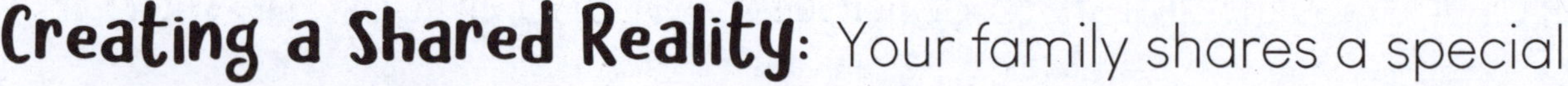

Creating a Shared Reality: Your family shares a special bond where everyone understands each other's thoughts and feelings. This is called a **Family Shared Social Reality (FSSR)**. To achieve FSSR, family members need to see things in a similar way, believe in each other's opinions and understand each other's feelings.

What Is Shared Reality?

A shared reality is like having a special map that guides us through our family adventures. It's like having a secret language that only the family understands.

How Do Families Create a Shared Reality?

Creating a shared reality is about building a sense of understanding and connection. Families use two special tools called conversation and conformity to build it together.

1. Conversation Orientation: Family meetings where everyone gets to share their thoughts and feelings about values, dreams and even daily life. By listening to each other and sharing perspectives, we build a deeper understanding of each other.

2. Conformity Orientation: Certain rules or beliefs are set by a family member, like a parent. This helps the family stay united and makes sure we're all on the same page.

The Four Communication Patterns

Combining conversation and conformity creates four unique communication patterns.

1. Consensual Families:

These families balance both conversation and conformity. They talk openly about views and opinions, but also respect the decisions made by the parents or other authority figures.

2. Protective Families:

In these families, conformity is key. Children are expected to trust the parents' decisions and follow their lead without discussion.

3. Pluralistic Families: These families focus mainly on conversation. They love sharing thoughts and ideas, and there's not much emphasis on conforming to a single viewpoint.

4. Laissez-Faire Families: In these families, neither conversation nor conformity are emphasized. They're all free to do their own thing, and there's not much structure or communication.

The Magic of Shared Reality

Once upon a time, in a bustling neighborhood in India, there lived four families who were the best of friends. Each family had its own unique way of communicating, and together, they formed a vibrant mix of shared realities.

First, there was the Sharma family. Mr. and Mrs. Sharma, along with their children Aarav and Meera, belonged to a Consensual family. Their home was always filled with lively discussions and debates. Every evening, they gathered around the dinner table, sharing stories of their day and expressing their opinions on various topics. While Mr. Sharma made the final decisions, he always made sure to listen to everyone before reaching a conclusion.

Next door lived the Singh family. Mr. and Mrs. Singh, along with their daughter Ananya, were part of a Protective family. In their home, rules were strictly enforced, and decisions were made by Mr. Singh, the head of the household. While there wasn't much room for discussion, the family members respected and trusted his judgment. They believed in following traditions and values passed down through generations.

On the other side of the street lived the Patel family. Mr. and Mrs. Patel, along with their son Rohan, belonged to a Pluralistic family. Their home was a haven of freedom and creativity. Everyone was encouraged to express themselves openly, and there were no strict rules to adhere to. The Patels

celebrated diversity of thought and encouraged each family member to pursue their interests and passions.

Finally, there was the Gupta family. Mr. and Mrs. Gupta, along with their daughter Priya, were part of a Laissez-Faire family. In their home, there was a sense of independence and autonomy. Each family member did their own thing, without much interference from others. While they loved each other dearly, they also valued their personal space and freedom.

Despite their different communication patterns, the four families were the best of friends. They respected each other's differences and celebrated their shared values of love, friendship and unity. Every evening, they would gather in the park, sharing laughter and stories as they watched the sun set behind the trees. In their own unique way, they had created a shared reality.

Why Does It Matter?

Having a shared reality helps families get along better and solve problems together. When everyone is on the same page, there's less conflict and more joy together! But sometimes, it can be tricky, especially when family members have different ideas or when kids want more independence.

1. Strengthening Bonds: Just like a sturdy rope is made of many threads, strong family bonds are woven from shared experiences and mutual understanding. When we create a shared reality, we reinforce these bonds, making our family connections even stronger.

2. Fostering Communication: Communication is the heartbeat of any family. When we create a shared reality, we open up channels of communication, allowing thoughts and feelings to flow freely. This creates an environment where everyone feels heard and valued, leading to deeper and more meaningful connections.

3. Resolving Conflicts: Resolving conflicts in our families is a bit like fitting two puzzle pieces together. It requires patience, understanding and the right approach to make things click. When we have a shared reality, we're better equipped to navigate disagreements and find solutions that work for everyone.

4. Nurturing Growth:

Just as a sapling needs water and sunlight to grow, family members need understanding and support to thrive. When we create a shared reality, we create an environment where everyone feels safe to be themselves and pursue their dreams.

5. Cultivating a Sense of Belonging:

Like pieces of a puzzle coming together to form a beautiful picture, creating a shared reality helps us feel a sense of belonging within our families. When we understand each other's values and perspectives, we feel connected and accepted for who we are.

By nurturing our connections, encouraging open communication, resolving conflicts with empathy, promoting growth and cultivating a sense of belonging, we create a harmonious and joyful family life that enriches our hearts and souls.

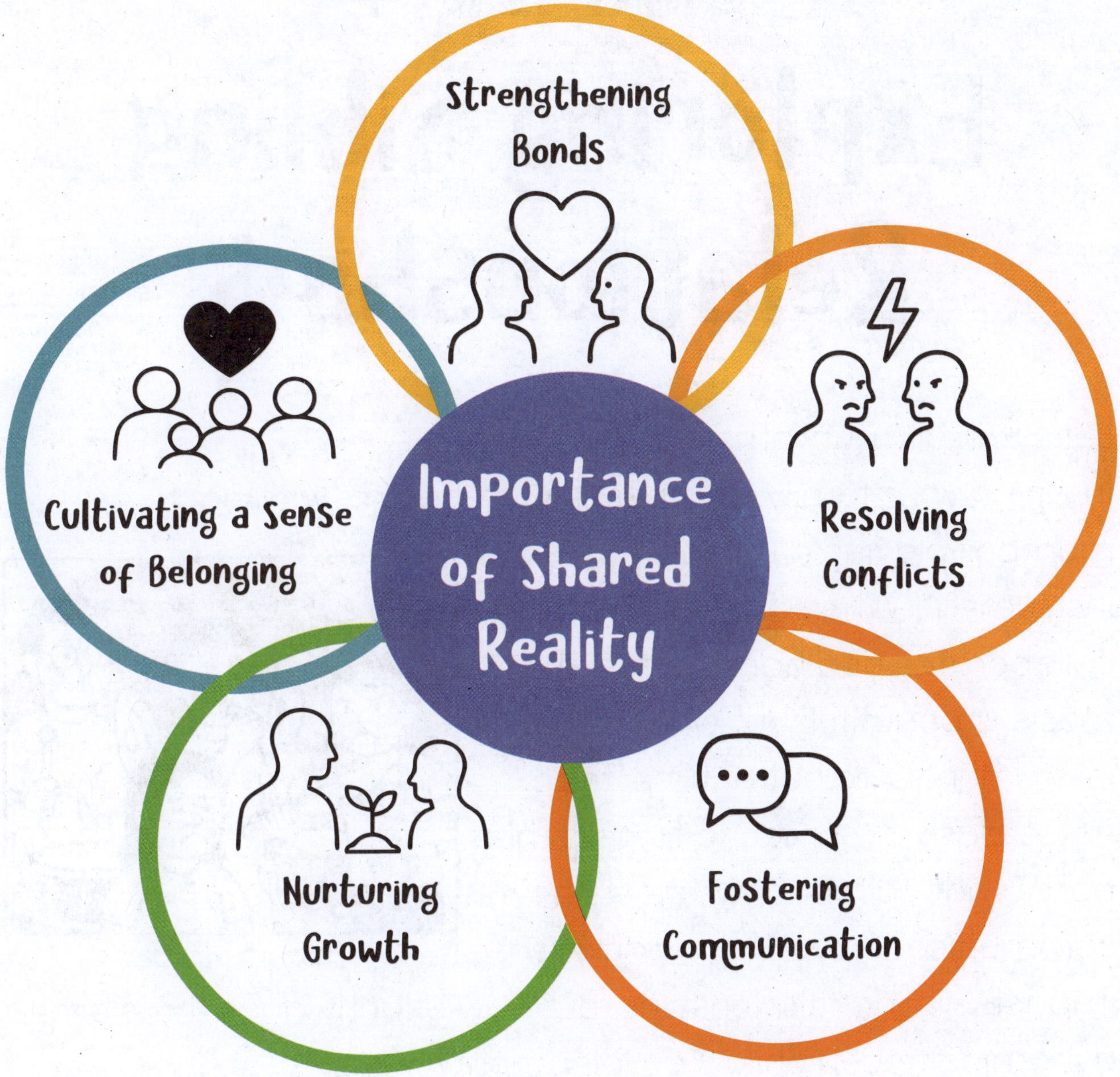
Importance of Shared Reality
Strengthening Bonds
Resolving Conflicts
Fostering Communication
Nurturing Growth
Cultivating a Sense of Belonging

ANXIETY

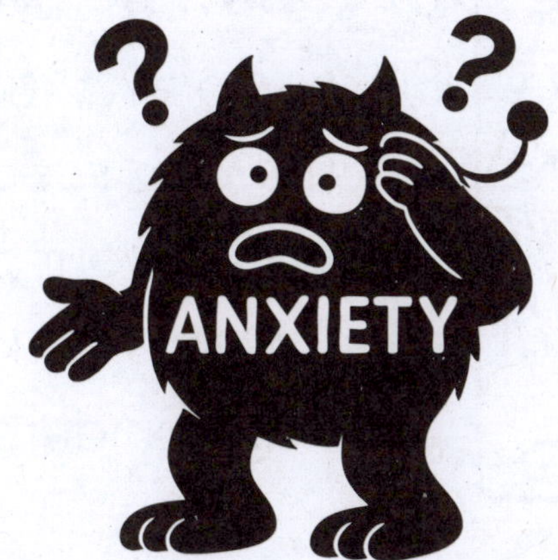

CHAPTER 4

Exploring Sibling Relationships

Let's talk about brothers and sisters!
Imagine your family as a bustling orchestra, with each member playing a unique instrument. When everyone listens, collaborates and harmonizes, the music is beautiful. But what if the instruments are out of tune, the notes clash or someone forgets their part? That cacophony reflects how communication, or the lack thereof, impacts sibling relationships. But how exactly does this sibling dynamic affect a child's development?

Beyond the Squabbles

Siblings aren't just rivals for toys or annoying roommates. They're co-stars in your personal development story, playing a key role in how you grow and understand the world.

1. Emotional Literacy: As siblings share countless experiences, they become experts at deciphering emotions, reading nonverbal cues and understanding each other's perspectives. This "emotional literacy" superpower transcends the family, allowing children to build strong friendships and navigate complex group dynamics and social situations with empathy and understanding.

2. Conflict Resolution: Sibling squabbles are actually training grounds for negotiation, compromise and finding win-win solutions. These "conflict resolution" skills equip children to handle future disagreements with confidence and grace, whether with classmates, friends or even future bosses.

3. Emotional Intelligence: Sharing joys, sorrows and everything in between with a sibling creates a safe space for exploring emotions. Children learn to express themselves authentically, manage their feelings constructively, build resilience in the face of challenges and develop a healthy emotional vocabulary.

4. Teacher and Student: Siblings often play the roles of teacher and student, pushing each other to learn and grow. Younger ones learn by observing and imitating older siblings, while older ones solidify their understanding by explaining and teaching. This fosters adaptability, curiosity and problem-solving skills.

5. Teamwork: Building blanket forts and battling imaginary dragons are rehearsals for teamwork! Siblings teach each other how to cooperate, share resources, take turns and support each other toward a common goal. This becomes invaluable in group projects, sports teams and even future careers.

6. Communication: Younger siblings often imitate the older child's language and actions during play, establishing shared meanings and fostering communication skills. This helps articulate thoughts and feelings effectively, building strong communication skills that benefit them in all aspects of life.

Remember, the music of your sibling relationship is a continuous performance, not a one-time act. There will be off-key moments, missed notes and even the occasional clash of cymbals. But with patience and understanding, you and your sibling can transform your family orchestra into a beautiful, harmonious symphony.

CHAPTER 5

Exploring Personal Relationships

Imagine you're on a thrilling adventure, but you're blindfolded. You can hear the sounds around you, feel the ground beneath your feet and sense the wind in your hair, but you can't see where you're going. That's what life can feel like when you don't communicate with yourself. You experience all sorts of emotions, but you might not fully understand what they mean or how to handle them. This is where **Emotional Ability Resources (EaR)** come in.

Think of **EaR** as a personal toolbox filled with different resources to help understand, navigate and ultimately master emotions. Just like any other skill, emotional intelligence needs practice and time to develop, and **EaR** can build this crucial skill.

Here's how this **Superpower** can help you grow in amazing ways.

1. Become a Master of Your Emotions:

Communicating with yourself is like having a whole toolbox full of amazing tools to help you manage your emotions. By listening to your feelings and needs, you can learn healthy coping mechanisms, like taking deep breaths, talking to a trusted adult or doing something fun and relaxing when you're overwhelmed.

2. Be Your Own Best Friend:

By communicating with yourself using kind and encouraging words, you become your own best friend. You can tell yourself things like, "You're capable and strong" or "It's okay to feel this way," just like you would comfort a friend who's going through a tough time. This positive self-talk builds your confidence and helps you navigate challenges with a smile.

3. Build Strong and Meaningful Relationships:

When you can recognize and express your feelings in a healthy way, it becomes easier to connect with others. You can share how you're feeling with friends and family, and they'll feel more comfortable sharing their feelings too!

CHAPTER 6

When and Where to Seek Help

It's totally normal to feel worried sometimes, but if it starts to interfere with daily life, reach out for help. Whether it's talking to a trusted adult or seeking support from a counselor, there's always someone ready to lend a listening ear and help you navigate those choppy waters of worry!

Here Are Some Signs to Look Out For:

1. Excessive Worry: Do you find yourself super-duper worried all the time? Are you feeling anxious often?

2. Daily Activities: Does worry get in the way of you doing activities or playing games you usually enjoy? Like going to school, hanging out with friends or even eating and sleeping well?

If you nodded yes to any of these, it might be a good idea to talk to someone.

So, who can you reach out to for support? Well, your parents are the first. They can listen to you, understand what's going on and guide you in the right direction. But if you're feeling nervous about talking to them or if they're not available, don't worry! Your school is also a fantastic place to turn to. They have special helpers who know all about feelings and worries and are trained to help you feel better.

Remember, it's perfectly okay to ask for help when you need it. There are plenty of caring people out there who want to support you and help you feel happier and more at ease!

CHAPTER 7

How to Respond

As a kid, you know the jitterbug and the butterfly better than most adults. Sometimes, when you're feeling anxious, adults might say things like "Don't worry!" or "Calm down!" But those words, even if they're meant to help, can feel as sour as a lemon!

It's important to remember that everyone's jitterbug and butterfly are different. What makes your heart race might not even make your friend blink! So, when adults say "relax," it might feel like they're speaking a different language.

But you can help them understand. The next time the jitterbug jitters or the butterfly flutters in your tummy, talk to a grown-up you trust. Tell them your tummy feels like a washing machine on high-spin or your thoughts are racing faster than a cheetah on roller skates. The more they know, the better they can help!

And remember, you're not alone. Lots of kids have both the jitterbug and the butterfly visit sometimes. And even grown-ups do too! The important thing is finding ways to soothe the grumpy butterfly, like taking deep breaths that smell like your favorite cookies, talking to someone who makes you laugh or doing something you love, like painting or building an epic fort.

Your Words Matter

Your words are like magic spells, each one carrying a special power. Some words can make you feel warm and happy, like sunshine on your face. Others can leave you feeling cold and sad, like a rainstorm chilling your bones.

For example, saying things like "calm down" or "don't worry" might sound helpful, but they can feel dismissive, like someone waving away a magic wand without really understanding the problem.

Instead, try using magic words that soothe and comfort. Saying "I'm here for you" or "What's bothering you?" creates a safe space for them to share their worries.

Here Are Some Magic Words You Can Use:

1. **"I hear you."** This shows you're really listening and care about their feelings.

2. **"What can I do to help?"** This lets them know you're willing to support them.

3. **"You're not alone."** This reminds them that everyone experiences anxiety sometimes.

4. **"You are brave."** This encourages them to face their fears with courage.

5. **"Would you like to talk about it?"** This opens the door for them to share if they're ready.

I can do this.

You can do this.

Section 3

Strategies for Anxiety

CHAPTER 1

Build Resilience and Manage Anxiety

Let's dive into the world of resilience and discover some cool exercises to help you feel calm and confident!

What Is Resilience?

Resilience is like having a magical shield that protects you during tough times. It helps you bounce back from challenges and keeps you strong and brave. Whether you're dealing with changes at school, big feelings or anything else that feels tricky, resilience is your secret weapon.

EaR Exercises to Build Resilience

1. Breathing: Take a deep breath in through your nose, imagining you're breathing in superpowers. Hold it for a moment, feeling your chest fill up like a balloon. Then slowly exhale through your mouth, imagining you're blowing away any worries or fears.

2. Mindful Moments: Find a quiet space where you can sit comfortably. Close your eyes and pay attention to your breathing. Notice how your chest rises and falls with each breath. Then imagine you're floating on a fluffy cloud, surrounded by peace and tranquility.

3. Positive Power-Ups: Think of three things that make you feel happy or proud. It could be playing your favorite game, spending time with a friend or achieving something awesome. Write them down or draw pictures of them in your journal.

4. Problem-Solving Quest:

Whenever you face a challenge, turn it into an exciting quest! Grab a piece of paper and draw a map of your adventure, with the challenge as your ultimate goal. Then brainstorm different ways you can overcome the challenge and write them down on your map. As you try out each solution, mark it on your map like a true adventurer.

5. Gratitude: Take a moment to think about three things you're grateful for today. Write them down in your gratitude journal and decorate the page with colorful drawings or stickers. Whenever you're feeling worried or stressed, read through the list to remind yourself of all the good things in your life.

Remember, you have the power within you to face any challenge with courage and strength. Keep practicing these exercises, believe in yourself and never forget that you're capable of amazing things.

It's okay to have Emotions

CHAPTER 2

Mindfulness

Story of Saisha

Saisha was an 8-year-old girl who hated school. All her friends made fun of her brown eyes, black hair and called her "Pingu." She feared losing her friends, so she would let them tease her and pretend it didn't bother her. She neither asserted herself nor asked them, gently but firmly, to stop making fun of her body. Since she did not love her body, she believed others had the right to comment on it.

She usually cried after school and then stuffed herself with the pasta that was always kept in the refrigerator for her. Food became a source of comfort for her. It relaxed her mind and calmed her. It helped her forget about her worries for a while.

Saisha thought that if her mother stayed at home instead of going to work, like Reena's mother, she would be happy and life would be good. So, she would wait quietly each day for her mom to come home.

Anxiety visits us when we worry too much. It flourishes when there is a sense of helplessness and a perception of loss of control over what is going on, when we do not trust our ability to manage a situation properly.

Because of anxiety, we tend to overeat or stop eating altogether. Because of anxiety, we feel unable to deal with certain situations. Because of anxiety, we struggle to remain calm and focus on the present. We go into the past to remember something which has already happened. Or imagine something happening in the future.

So, to deal with any situation, we need to remain in the present. When we focus on the present, anxiety starts to disappear slowly. It feels similar to what we see in the sky every morning, every dawn. Bit by bit, there is no darkness left after the sun appears.

So, What Can Help Us Stay in the Present?

Drawing our attention to something that is in the here and now, like breathing. Take deep, slow breaths and count them to come back to the present moment. This practice of being aware and conscious is called mindfulness.

Let's learn deep breathing as a mindfulness activity to build your emotional strength and increase emotional ability. Follow these steps to practice mindful breathing:

1. Find a Comfortable Space: Sit or lie down in a comfortable position with your back straight and shoulders relaxed. You can close your eyes if you wish.

2. Focus on Your Breath: Pay attention to the sensation of your breath entering and leaving your body. Feel your abdomen rise and fall with each breath.

3. Inhale Slowly and Deeply: Breathe in slowly through your nose while counting to five.

4. Hold Your Breath: Briefly hold your breath, if you can.

5. Exhale Slowly and Completely: Exhale slowly through your mouth or nose while counting to five.

6. Repeat: Repeat the steps for several minutes, focusing on the sensation of your breath and the calming effect it has on your body and mind.

Regular practice makes us good at things. If your mind wanders, gently bring your attention back to your breath. You can adjust the length of your inhalations and exhalations as needed. Set aside five minutes every day to do it. Over time, you will be able to do it automatically, even in difficult situations.

Star Breathing

Start at any "Breathe in" side, hold your breath at the tip, then breathe out. Keep going until you've gone around the whole star.

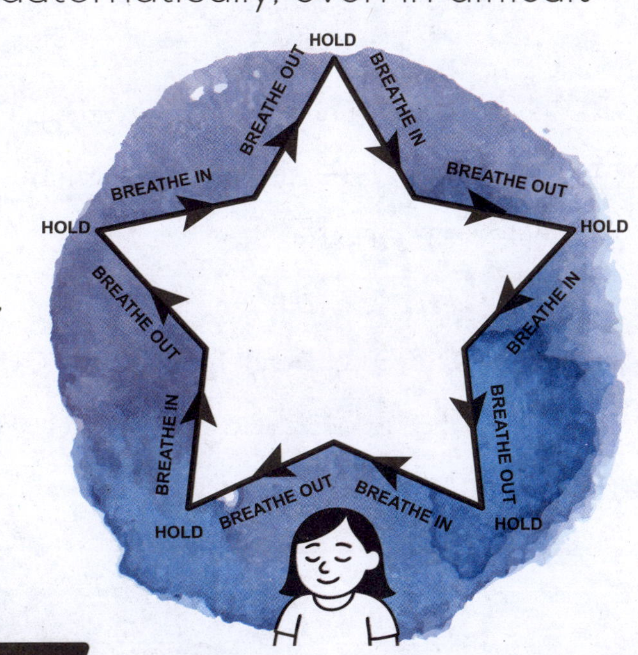

CHAPTER 3

EaR Techniques

Help yourself become more mindful with these engaging exercises and strengthen your emotional resilience.

Become a Mighty Tree:

1. Imagine transforming yourself into a mighty tree, strong and grounded. Take off your shoes and feel the earth beneath your bare feet, like roots anchoring you to the ground.

2. Close your eyes and visualize strong roots growing from your feet, burrowing deep into the earth's core.

3.Take slow, deep breaths, feeling your tummy rise and fall like the gentle swaying of leaves in the breeze.

4. Picture a strong wind blowing, but your roots hold you steady, reminding you of your inner strength.

5. Open your eyes and wiggle your toes, feeling the renewed connection with the earth.

Breathing Buddy:

1. Find your beloved stuffed animal or toy and become "breathing buddies." Lie down comfortably and place your buddy on your belly.

2. Close your eyes and focus on the gentle rise and fall of your belly, mirroring the movement of your buddy as you breathe in and out together.

3. Feel the calmness spread through you with each breath, like sunshine warming the earth.

The Fox Walk:

1. Transform your backyard or park into a nature exploration zone. Take off your shoes and socks, feeling the grass or earth beneath your toes, and embark on a mindful journey.

2. Walk slowly and quietly, like a fox, focusing on the sensation of each step. Feel your heel touch the ground first, then the roll of your foot, followed by the gentle press of your toes.

3. Become a keen listener, and pay attention to the chirping of birds, the rustling of leaves and the gentle breeze whispering through the trees. Notice how these sounds can calm your mind and spirit.

Body Scan:

1. Find a quiet, comfortable spot and lie down. Close your eyes and take a few deep breaths, letting your worries drift away like clouds in the sky.

2. Gently focus your awareness on different parts of your body, starting with your toes and slowly moving up. Notice any sensations you experience.

3. Allow your body to completely unwind and embrace the calmness of the moment.

Supercharge Your Day with EaR Techniques!

Ready to use your techniques every day?

1. Pick Your Favorite:

Think of these techniques like different games. Choose the one you like best, whether it's like playing the "Mighty Tree" or being a "Breathing Buddy" with your stuffed animal.

2. 21-Day Challenge:

Pretend you're on a 21-day adventure! Try doing your chosen technique every day for 21 days, just like brushing your teeth! It helps turn it into a fun habit.

Embrace your feelings

FEAR
JOY
SADNESS
WORRY
GRIEF
ANGER
SHAME
ANXIETY

3. Keep Going:

Remember, practice makes perfect! If you miss a day, don't worry, just jump back in the next day.

4. Use This Page as Your Log!

You can mark each day you do your technique. It serves as a reminder and shows how you're doing!

	Day	Date	Time (morning, noon, evening)	No. of times performed
1				
2				
3				
4				
5				
6				
7				
8				
9				
10				
11				
12				

	Day	Date	Time (morning, noon, evening)	No. of times performed
13				
14				
15				
16				
17				
18				
19				
20				
21				

CHAPTER 4

Calm the Storm

Have you ever felt like a volcano about to erupt? Maybe your tummy's in knots, your heart's racing like a drum solo and your mind's filled with worries. Fear not, here are some calming strategies for you!

What Is a Calming Strategy?

It's a special way to help your body and mind relax when you're feeling overwhelmed. It can be anything from taking deep breaths to squeezing a stress ball.

When we're anxious, our bodies feel tense and it's hard to focus on things. Calming strategies are like training wheels for our emotions. They help us steady ourselves, calm down and face challenges.

1. Cozy Corner: Create a special space in your room with calming objects like fluffy pillows, soothing music and your favorite books. When you need to relax, take a few minutes in your cozy corner to unwind.

2. Calming Creative: Draw, paint, write or build something to express your emotions. Creating something can be a great way to release tension and feel calmer.

3. Sensory Superhero: Listen to calming music, take a warm bath or snuggle with a soft blanket. These sensory experiences can be very soothing and promote relaxation.

4. Squeezy Squad: Keep a stress ball or a squishy toy near you. When you feel anxious, squeeze it! This can help release tension and refocus your mind.

5. Positive Thinking: When you start to worry, replace negative thoughts with positive affirmations like "I am calm," "I am capable" or "I can handle this."

Remember, these are just some ideas, and the best calming strategies are the ones that work best for you! So, experiment, find what works for you and become a master of managing your anxieties.

What Can I Do When I Feel Anxious?

I Can...

Have water or snacks

Ask for a hug

Read a book

Use a fidget toy

Hug a teddy

Play some building games

Do little deep breathing exercises

Work on a puzzle

Talk to mom or dad

_________________________ (Add your own idea!)

(TAKE WHATEVER YOU NEED TO HEAR RIGHT NOW)

IT'S OKAY TO FEEL:

OVERWHELMED

UNSURE

EXHAUSTED

ANXIOUS

UNFULLFILLED

SAD

CHAPTER 5

Self-Love

We've explored what anxiety is, tackled communication strategies to manage it and even learned some calming techniques. But there's another powerful weapon in our arsenal, called self-love.

Let's discover how embracing our unique selves can be the ultimate antidote to anxiety. Loving and appreciating ourselves fuels our confidence, reduces self-doubt and empowers us to face challenges with greater resilience.

Self-love acts as a strong foundation, making us less vulnerable to the attacks of anxiety.

Here's How Self-Love Works:

1. Building Self-Esteem: When you love yourself, you start accepting and appreciating your unique qualities, strengths and even your flaws. This builds a strong sense of self-worth, making you less susceptible to negative self-talk and external criticisms.

2. Boosting Self-Confidence: When you love yourself, you trust your abilities and believe in yourself. You're more likely to take risks, face challenges head-on and bounce back from setbacks. This confidence acts as a buffer against anxiety by reducing fear of failure.

3. Banishing Negative Thoughts: When you love yourself, you become less susceptible to negative self-talk and harmful comparisons with others. These negative thoughts often fuel anxiety and make even small challenges seem overwhelming.

Remember, self-love is a journey, not a destination. It takes time and effort, but the results are worth it. You've got this!

Self-Love Acts

1. Positive Talk: When you look in the mirror, say something nice to yourself, like "I look great today!" or "I'm super smart."

2. Take Care of Yourself: Treat yourself like a precious treasure. Eat yummy, healthy foods, get enough rest and play a lot.

3. Celebrate Small Wins: When you do something cool, like finishing a puzzle or helping a friend, celebrate it! You can even give yourself a little high-five.

4. Forgive Mistakes: Nobody's perfect, and that's okay! If you make a mistake, forgive yourself and learn from it.

5. Be Your Own Best Friend: Imagine you're your best friend. How would you treat yourself? Do that!

Emotion Jar

every feeling counts!

Here is another technique that you can use daily to incorporate self-love. Affirmations are like friendly reminders that can help boost your self-love.

1. I am unique and special just the way I am.
2. I love and accept myself, flaws and all.
3. I am kind and treat others with respect.
4. I am brave and can face any challenge.
5. I am smart and capable of learning new things.
6. I am surrounded by love and support from family and friends.
7. I am worthy of happiness and success.
8. I am a good friend who cares for others.
9. I am in charge of my thoughts and choose to think positively.
10. I am confident in who I am and what I can do.
11. I am grateful for the good things in my life.
12. I am strong and can handle tough times with courage.

13. I am loved just as I am, no matter what.

14. I am responsible for my own happiness and can make choices that make me feel good.

15. I am growing and learning every day.

Repeat these affirmations to yourself, especially when you're feeling down or unsure.

CHAPTER 6

The Power of Journaling

Journaling, the simple act of putting pen to paper, is more than just recording events or thoughts. It's a powerful tool for self-discovery, expression and, most importantly, managing anxiety.

What Is Journaling?

At its core, journaling is a personal and reflective recording of your thoughts, feelings and experiences. It's a space where you can be completely honest and unfiltered, without judgment or pressure. Unlike essays or formal writing, there are no rules or expectations. You can write in any style, format or language that feels comfortable to you.

Why Journaling?

Journaling offers a multitude of benefits for our mental and emotional well-being. Here are a few key reasons to consider making it a regular habit:

1. Increased Self-Awareness: By writing down your thoughts and feelings, you gain a clearer understanding of what's going on inside your mind. You can identify recurring patterns, triggers and emotions you might not have been aware of.

2. Improved Emotional Processing: Journaling provides a safe space to express difficult emotions, allowing you to process them in a healthy way. Bottling up emotions can lead to further stress and anxiety, while expressing them through writing can be cathartic and liberating.

3. Enhanced Creativity: Journaling can spark creative thinking and unlock new ideas. By exploring your thoughts freely, you might discover solutions to problems you've been struggling with.

4. Boost in Memory: Writing down information helps you retain it better. Journaling can be a valuable tool for learning and remembering new things.

Why Is Journaling Especially Beneficial for You?

Have you ever stopped to notice how many thoughts zoom around in your head like buzzing bees in a garden? Sometimes, they can feel like a swirling storm. Imagine your journal as a magical book, just for you. Inside its colorful pages, you can write anything and everything that pops into your head.

1. Your Own Happy Island: Feeling down? Write about the things that make you smile, like your best friend's infectious laugh, the sweet smell of grandma's cookies or the way sunshine warms your face.

2. A Worry Whisperer: Sometimes, big problems can feel like scary monsters under your bed. Let your journal be your superhero cape! Write down your worries and watch them shrink to the size of ants as you face them head-on.

3. A Creativity Explosion: Feeling like an artist bursting with ideas? Unleash your inner Picasso! Use your journal to draw funny faces, write poems about fluffy clouds or even design your own superhero costume!

4. A Super-Sleuth's Notebook: Did something tricky happen at school? Write it down like a detective gathering clues. Brainstorm ideas to solve the mystery.

There are no rules! You can write in any way you like, silly or serious, long or short, with colorful pictures or neat handwriting. The only rule is to have fun and be yourself.

The more you use your journal, the more you'll discover its powers. You might learn surprising things about yourself, unlock incredible ideas and even become a better friend!

What Did You Do Today? How Did You Feel?

Write all about your days for a week, and don't forget to be honest with yourself. Remember, your journal is your safe space to express yourself freely!

ANXIETY

ANXIETY

ANXIETY

ANXIETY

ANXIETY

ANXIETY

Section 4

People Around Me

CHAPTER 1
Parents

Meet Sid, an 8-year-old boy, and his dad, Sanjay. Lately, Sid has been having problems concentrating on his studies. He worries a lot about completing his homework and has been feeling butterflies in his stomach every time his dad asks him to go out to parties with him or whenever they have many guests at home. Sanjay decides it's time for Sid to seek help from a therapist. The therapist not only works with Sid but also talks to Sanjay about how parents can sometimes make their children's anxiety worse, without even knowing it.

When kids get anxious, parents can feel worried too. It's natural for parents to want to protect their kids, but sometimes, their own worries can make things trickier. Sanjay might feel stressed when he sees Sid anxious, and that's okay! But sometimes, this stress can make parents react in a way that doesn't help their kids feel better.

How Parents' Actions Affect Anxiety

Some things parents do can make anxiety hang around longer, while others can help it go away.

Let's Break It Down

1. Overdoing It: Sometimes, parents might get too involved in their kids' lives, trying to control everything they do. This can make anxiety stick around longer.

2. Reassurance Overload: When parents keep telling their kids everything's okay, even when it's not, it can make anxiety hang around like an unwanted guest.

3. Avoiding the Problem: If parents let their kids skip things that make them anxious, it might feel better in the moment, but it doesn't teach them how to face their fears.

4. Showing Anxiety: If parents seem anxious themselves, it can make their kids feel more anxious too. It's like catching a case of the nerves!

5. Feeling Helpless: When parents act like there's nothing they can do to help, it can make anxiety seem scarier than it really is.

6. Not Doing Anything: If parents ignore their kids' anxiety, hoping it'll go away on its own, it might stick around longer than expected.

7. Being Negative: No one likes to hear mean stuff, especially from their parents! If parents criticize or blame their kids for feeling anxious, it can make them feel even worse.

Parental Beliefs and Attitudes

Let's consider the significant role of **parental beliefs and attitudes**. Their belief system is shaped by their own experiences and values, and in turn, these beliefs shape their attitudes, influencing their expectations, communication and parenting style. Parents who believe in honesty might have a strict approach to truth-telling, while those who value creativity might encourage their child to explore imaginative avenues.

1. "My child needs to be perfect."

This can make kids feel pressured to succeed all the time, leading to anxiety and fear of failure. It can also discourage kids from trying new things, as they might worry about making mistakes.

2. "My child shouldn't express negative emotions." This can make kids feel like they need to bottle up their feelings, leading to emotional outbursts or difficulty managing difficult emotions later in life.

3. "My child needs constant praise and rewards." While encouragement is important, relying solely on praise and rewards can make kids less motivated when those things aren't available. It's better to help them feel proud of their own efforts.

4. "My child should obey me without question." While there are times when setting limits is necessary, encouraging open communication and explaining the reasons behind rules can help kids develop their own sense of right and wrong.

5. "My child is incapable or needs to be saved."

Underestimating a child's abilities can hold them back from learning and growing. It's important to trust kids to try new things, make mistakes and learn from those experiences.

These ideas, like skilled hands shaping clay, can profoundly impact child development.

1. Internalization: Children are highly susceptible to the beliefs and attitudes they are exposed to. A parent who believes in fairness might inadvertently instill this value in their child, influencing their interactions with peers.

2. Behavioral Guidance:
Parental attitudes guide behavior. Encouraging exploration with a positive attitude can motivate children to try new things, while a critical attitude toward mistakes might discourage them from taking risks.

3. Confidence Building: When parents express belief in their child's potential and have a supportive attitude toward their aspirations, it fosters a sense of self-efficacy, empowering them to pursue their dreams.

However, it's crucial to remember that you are not simply a passive product of your environment. You play an active role in shaping your own identity. Your unique experiences, thoughts and choices contribute significantly to shaping who you become.

CHAPTER 2

Teachers

Ayan is a bright and friendly student in Ms. Ayesha's fourth-grade class. He loves learning new things and enjoys spending time with his friends during recess. However, lately, Ayan has been feeling more and more hesitant about speaking up in class.

Ms. Ayesha assigns a class project where each student has to give a short presentation about their favorite book. Ayan's heart races just thinking about standing up in front of his classmates and talking. He worries that he'll forget what to say or that everyone will laugh at him.

As the presentation day approaches, Ayan's worries grow bigger. He starts to feel sick to his stomach and has trouble sleeping at night. His mom notices that he's been quieter than usual and asks him what's wrong, but Ayan brushes it off, not wanting to worry her.

On the main day, Ayan's anxiety is at its peak. When it's his turn to speak, he freezes. Ms. Ayesha notices that Ayan looks distressed and gently encourages him to take a deep breath and try again. She reminds him that it's okay to feel nervous and that everyone makes mistakes sometimes.

Instead of pressuring Ayan to continue, Ms. Ayesha offers him the option to present in front of a smaller group or privately after class. Ayan feels relieved knowing that he has other options and decides to give it another try with Ms. Ayesha's support.

Afterward, Ayan feels proud of himself for facing his fear, even though it was tough. Ms. Ayesha praises him for his bravery and assures him that she's always there to help him whenever he needs it.

Anxiety at School

Did you know that, sometimes, feelings like worry or nervousness can follow you to school? It can sneak into your backpack and come along for the ride. But don't worry, there are teachers to help.

Understanding the Role of Teachers

Teachers are like the guardians of knowledge in school, but they're also guardians of your feelings. They know that sometimes, kids feel a little jittery or scared, and they're ready to lend a helping hand.

Teachers: More Than Just Educators

Teachers are like the captains of our school ship. They guide us through the sea of knowledge and help us navigate the ups and downs of learning. They don't just teach math and science; they also teach empathy, kindness and understanding.

1. Seeing Beyond the Surface: When a student seems quiet or unsure, teachers often know there might be something going on beneath the surface. They understand that anxiety isn't always loud and obvious—it can be like a whisper, quietly nagging at you from the inside.

2. Every Kid Is Different: Just like how each snowflake is unique, every kid's experience with anxiety is different too. Teachers listen carefully, pay attention to your body language and try to understand what's going on inside your head.

3. A Big Emotion in a Small Package: Anxiety can be a big, overwhelming feeling packed into a small word. Teachers understand that even though anxiety might seem small, it can have a big impact on how you feel and act.

4. Invisible Battles: Sometimes, you might look fine on the outside, but inside, you might be struggling to keep those anxious thoughts at bay. Teachers know that it takes a lot of courage to face those invisible battles, and they're here to support you every step of the way.

5. Empathy and Understanding:

Teachers know that anxiety isn't something you can just switch off like a light. It's a complex mix of thoughts, feelings and worries that can be hard to shake off.

6. Creating a Safe Space:

In the classroom, teachers work hard to create a safe and supportive environment where every student feels valued and understood. They know that when you feel safe and loved, it's easier to face your fears and conquer your anxieties.

Helping or Hurting?

But sometimes, teachers might do things that unintentionally make anxiety feel bigger.

Letting You Skip Activities:

Imagine you're feeling really nervous about giving a presentation in front of the class. Your teacher notices and says, "It's okay, you don't have to do it if you're feeling anxious." While this might seem nice, it could also make anxiety stronger because you didn't get the chance to face your fear and see that you could do it!

Giving You Less Work: Sometimes, teachers might notice that you're feeling anxious and decide to give you less work to reduce pressure. They might think this will make things easier for you, but it could send a message that they don't believe you're capable of handling challenges.

Allowing Avoidance: If you're feeling anxious about a certain activity, like playing a game with your classmates, your teacher might let you sit out and do something else instead. While this might give you a break from anxiety in the moment, it doesn't help you learn how to cope with similar situations in the future.

Offering Too Much Reassurance: Your teacher might notice you're feeling anxious and try to reassure you by saying things like, "Don't worry, everything will be fine." While it's nice to hear comforting words, too much reassurance might make you feel like your teacher doesn't understand how big your anxiety feels.

Changing Classroom Environment: Sometimes, teachers might change the classroom environment to make it quieter or less busy if they know you're feeling anxious. While this might help in the short term, it doesn't teach you how to cope with different situations outside of school where things might not be as calm.

So, while teachers' intentions are usually good, it's important for them to understand that some actions might unintentionally make anxiety feel stronger. Instead, they can help by encouraging you to face your fears, offering support and being patient as you learn to cope with anxious feelings.

Things That Teachers Can Do When You're Anxious:

Notice and validate

Suggest a break

Guide breathing or grounding

Reduce pressure

CHAPTER 3

People Around Us

Have you ever heard someone say something that made you feel sad or upset, even though they didn't mean to? It happens to all of us sometimes. But did you know that some things people say can unintentionally hurt those who have anxiety?

Now, imagine you're feeling really worried or scared about something, and you share your feelings with someone you trust. Instead of listening and understanding, they say something that makes you feel even worse. Ouch! That's what it can feel like for people with anxiety when they hear certain comments.

Let's explore some of the things people say to those with anxiety and why these comments can hurt. We'll also learn how to choose our words carefully and show empathy for those who are struggling with anxiety.

1. "Other people have it worse than you."

Imagine you're feeling sad or scared, and someone tells you

that other people have bigger problems. It might make you feel like your feelings don't matter. Everyone's struggles are valid, no matter how big or small they may seem.

2. "You shouldn't rely on medication."

Sometimes, people with anxiety need medication to help them feel better, just how you might need medicine when you're sick. Saying they shouldn't rely on medication can make them feel like their struggles aren't real or important.

3. "You're making a mountain out of a molehill."

This saying means someone is making a big deal out of something small. But for someone with anxiety, even small things can feel really scary. It's important to remember that everyone's fears are different, and what seems small to one person might feel huge to another.

4. "Everybody feels stressed sometimes."

When someone shares their feelings of anxiety, telling them that everyone feels stressed can make them feel like their struggles aren't valid. It's important to listen to their feelings without comparing them to others'.

5. "Just calm down."

Imagine you're feeling really scared, and someone tells you to just calm down. It might make you feel like they don't understand how hard it is to control your feelings when you're anxious. Sometimes, it's not that easy to calm down, even if we want to.

6. "Again?"

Hearing "again?" when you tell someone that you're anxious can make you feel like they don't understand how hard it is to deal with anxiety. It's important to be supportive and understanding, even if someone's anxiety comes up often.

7. "You need to change your mindset."

Telling someone to change their mindset when they're anxious can make them feel like their struggles are their fault. It's not easy to change how we think, especially when anxiety makes everything feel scary.

The Worried Dragon and Words That Hurt

Have you ever met a dragon? Not a fire-breathing, princess-stealing kind, but a worried dragon named Willow. Willow wasn't scary at all, but sometimes, she felt like there was a storm brewing inside her, making her worry and fret about everything.

One day, while playing hide-and-seek with her friends, Willow felt the storm rumble. Her scales prickled, her heart thumped like a drum and her thoughts got all tangled up. Suddenly, she felt like she couldn't breathe!

When her friends found her, they tried to help. "Don't be silly, Willow," said one. "There's nothing to worry about!" Another chimed in, "Just calm down and take a deep breath."

But Willow's storm raged on. The words, though meant kindly, felt like tiny pinpricks, making her worry even worse. Tears welled up in her eyes, and she wished they could understand.

Just then, a wise old owl named Hoot saw what was happening. He landed softly beside Willow and asked gently, "What's troubling you, little one?" Willow sniffed and poured her heart out, explaining the storm inside her and how the things her friends had said made her feel worse. Hoot listened patiently, his kind eyes reflecting understanding.

"Remember, Willow," Hoot said softly, "the storm inside you doesn't make you weak. It just means you need a different kind of help." He explained that, sometimes, words like "just calm down" can feel dismissive, even though they come from a good place.

"What can I do then?" asked Willow, wiping her tears.

Hoot hooted gently. "The best thing you can do is tell your friends how their words make you feel. Maybe they didn't realize how they sounded. And remember, you're not alone. There are people who understand and can help you manage the storm inside."

So, Willow told her friends how their words made her feel. They listened carefully and learned some helpful ways to support Willow when she felt anxious. Now, when Willow feels anxious, they use better words, like "I'm here for you" and "How can I help?"

Remember, just like Willow, everyone experiences emotions differently. When someone you care about feels anxious, listen with an open heart, use kind words and offer support.

CHAPTER 4

Attachment

Feeling Safe with Those We Love

Attachment theory helps us understand the special bond between children and their primary caregivers. It was first talked about by a clever man named John Bowlby many years ago. He said that when babies feel safe and loved by their parents, they grow up to be happy and confident. But if they don't feel safe and loved, they might grow up to feel scared and unsure.

Let's dive into what attachment really means for us, from when we're little until we're all grown up.

What Is Attachment?

Attachment is like having a special connection with someone who cares for you. Think about your best friend or your favorite toy. You feel happy and safe when you're with them, right? That's because you're attached to them.

Why Attachment Matters?

Have you ever felt scared or worried when you couldn't find your parents in a crowded place? That's because you're attached to them, and you want them to be there when you need them.

This feeling of safety helps children explore the world around them and learn new things. But if they don't feel secure with their parents, they might feel anxious or scared, making it hard for them to explore and learn new things.

Different Types of Attachment

There are different types of attachment. Some kids feel really secure with their parents and know they can count on them. It is a secure attachment. Others might feel unsure if their parents will be there for them, so they get worried and anxious. It is an insecure attachment.

When we talk about attachment, we talk about the special bond between children and their caregivers. This bond plays a big role in how children feel and act as they grow up. There are different patterns of attachment, each with its own characteristics and effects on children's development.

1. Secure Attachment: Imagine a warm hug from your parents when you're feeling sad or scared. Children with secure attachment feel safe and loved, and are usually confident about the world around them. They explore and learn new things with enthusiasm because they know they have support.

2. Avoidant Attachment: Some children might seem independent and self-reliant, but deep down they might feel anxious or unsure about their parents' love and support. They avoid being close to their parents or showing their emotions because they're afraid of being rejected or getting hurt. These children often learn to rely on themselves and may have a hard time trusting others.

3. Resistant Attachment: Children with resistant attachment are always seeking reassurance and comfort from their parents, but no matter how much reassurance they get, it never seems like enough. These children might cling to their parents and have a hard time being apart from

them. This can make it difficult for them to explore and try new things on their own.

4. Disorganized Attachment: Children with disorganized attachment might seem confused or conflicted in their relationships with their parents. They might show a mix of behaviors, like seeking comfort one moment and pushing their parents away the next. These children often struggle with regulating their emotions and may show signs of stress or anxiety. They might have problems with aggression, self-esteem and social interactions.

It's important to remember that these attachment patterns are not permanent. They can change over time, especially with the help of supportive caregivers and positive experiences. Understanding attachment can help parents and caregivers provide the love and support children need to grow into happy, confident adults.

CHAPTER 5

Building a Caring Community

One sunny afternoon, Rohan, an 8-year-old, decided to gather his friends and start something exciting—a community club. He thought it would be fantastic if all the kids in the neighborhood could come together, make new friends and help each other in various ways.

Rohan's idea quickly caught on and they named it "The Sunshine Squad" because they wanted to bring sunshine to each other's lives.

Building a Community:

The Sunshine Squad started with weekly meetings, where they discussed their ideas for helping others and improving their neighborhood. They decided to organize clean-up days at the local park, plant flowers to make their streets more beautiful and even start a book exchange to share their favorite stories.

Rohan loved how the community club brought kids together and showed them the joy of working as a team. "When we help each other, we can do amazing things."

Challenge for You

Start by building a community where everyone feels welcome and valued.

Activity 1: Welcome New Friends

If someone new joins your class or moves into your neighborhood, create a "Welcome Squad" with your friends and make a colorful welcome card. Write friendly messages and draw fun pictures on it. Give the card to the new person with a warm smile to let them know they're part of your awesome community.

Activity 2: Share and Care

Organize a "Sharing Circle" with your friends. Everyone brings something special to share, like a favorite toy, a book or a snack. As you share, talk about why these things are important to you.

Playing Sports and Having Fun:

The Sunshine Squad wasn't just about helping others; they also loved playing sports together. Rohan was an excellent soccer player, and he taught his friends some cool soccer tricks.

Playing sports together helped the kids bond and stay healthy. It also showed them that teamwork on the field could lead to victories, just like teamwork in their community led to positive changes.

Activity 3: Include Everyone

Gather your friends for a game of tag, soccer or any fun game you enjoy. Before starting, make a rule that everyone gets a chance to play.

Activity 4: Cheer for Each Other

Next time you play a game or sport, make a "Cheer Poster" with encouraging messages like "Go, Team!" or "You're Amazing!" During the game, cheer for both teams, and if someone scores or makes a great move, give them a round of applause.

Activity 5: Be Fair

Create a list of "Fair Play Rules" with your friends. Include things like "play by the rules," "shake hands after the game" and "give three cheers for the opposing team."

Being Empathetic:

One day, Rohan noticed that one of his friends, Riya, seemed sad. Instead of ignoring it, he went up to her and asked if she was okay. She looked surprised but then shared her worries. Rohan listened carefully and offered her comfort.

Rohan's empathy showed everyone in The Sunshine Squad the importance of being there for each other, especially when someone needed a friend. They started a "Helping Hand"

program, where they pair up to support each other during challenging times.

Activity 6: Listen Actively

Gather with your friends in a circle and play the "Listening Game." One person talks about their day while the others listen without interrupting. Afterward, share what you learned about your friend's day.

Activity 7: Ask, Don't Assume

Create "Empathy Cards" with your friends. Each card has an emotion written on it, like "happy," "sad" or "worried." Take turns picking a card and sharing a time you felt that way. Listen to each other's stories, ask questions and learn about each other's emotions.

Activity 8: Offer Help

Organize a "Helping Hands" day with your friends. Together, decide on a helpful activity, like cleaning up a park, collecting toys for kids in need or making cards for senior citizens.

Rohan's belief that kids could make a difference by helping each other and building a close-knit community became a reality with The Sunshine Squad. Together, they learned that kindness, teamwork and empathy were like magic ingredients that could make their neighborhood a brighter and better place for everyone.

Guidance for Society

Mental Health Education: Society plays an important role in raising awareness about childhood anxiety. Communities can organize workshops and seminars through NGOs or government programs to educate parents, teachers and community members about recognizing and supporting anxious children.

Accessible Counseling Services: Communities can work together to make mental health services more accessible to families. School counselors and therapists can be made more accessible to provide support and guidance when needed.

Anti-Bullying Initiatives:

Our society as a whole needs to take a stand against bullying, which is a major source of anxiety for children. Schools can implement anti-bullying programs, and parents should be taught and encouraged to talk to their children about this issue.

CHAPTER 6

Whole Person Model

Amish, an 11-year-old boy living in a bustling city, was known for his academic excellence. However, the constant expectations from his parents and teachers often left him feeling anxious. The pressure to excel weighed heavily on his young shoulders, making him doubt his abilities.

One sunny afternoon, as Amish returned home from school, he noticed his heart racing and his palms sweaty. He recognized these physical symptoms of anxiety and realized the importance of paying more attention to his body. To combat this, he decided to incorporate short breaks, stretching, walks and deep breathing exercises into his daily routine. These simple actions helped him regain control over his anxiety.

Amish's emotional struggles came to a head one day during a particularly challenging math test. Overwhelmed and anxious, he decided to open up to his parents. "Mom, Dad, I'm really worried about this math test.

I'm scared I won't do well," he confessed. His parents listened attentively and assured him of their unwavering support, regardless of the test's outcome. This newfound openness allowed Amish to share his emotions with his family more often, and in doing so, some of his anxieties were alleviated.

In his pursuit of better mental well-being, Amish adopted a new approach to his studies. Rather than fixating on the uncertainty of the future, he learned to focus on the present moment. He reminded himself, "I'll do my best right now." This shift in mindset significantly reduced his anxiety about upcoming exams and assignments.

Amish's personal journey was influenced by his grandmother's wisdom. She once told him, "To be truly happy, you must love and accept yourself for who you are." These words stuck with him, prompting him to celebrate his achievements, no matter how minor. Over time, he began to develop a sense of self-worth.

He also learned the importance of social connections in managing anxiety and decided to become more involved with his peers. He joined a school club that aligned with his interests, which allowed him to form friendships with like-minded individuals. By actively listening and sharing his thoughts with others, he not only built meaningful relationships but also bolstered his self-confidence.

Amish's newfound ability to make choices was put to the test one day when he faced conflicting priorities. He had a significant school project to complete, but his friends invited him to play at the park. In the past, this decision would have caused him considerable stress. However, Amish calmly assessed the situation and thought, "I can choose to finish my project first, and then I'll have more fun at the park later." By effectively prioritizing his responsibilities while still allowing time for enjoyment, he showcased his improved decision-making skills.

At a young age, there are many expectations from parents, and you might feel like there's a lot of comparisons going on. Sometimes, you start thinking, "I'm not good enough," and when that feeling creeps in, it can be hard to manage yourself. But guess what? There's a way to help understand and handle all these feelings.

Imagine your feelings and thoughts like a wheel, a wheel that represents the "whole person model." It's a bit like your favorite toy, and every part of it is equally important. Just like how parents or teachers check specific things, in this wheel, you can't say that one segment is more important than the others. They all need to be balanced and work together for you to feel your best.

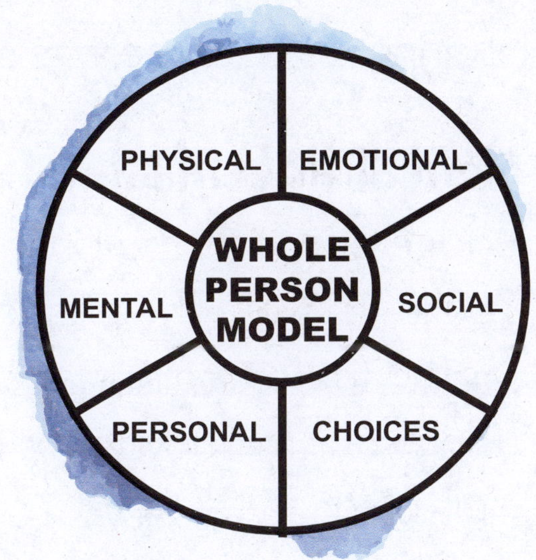

Let's break down the wheel into different segments to understand it better.

Physical Well-Being: Are you getting enough exercise? Are you taking care of your body and feeling comfortable in it? It's essential to have a good relationship with your body because it's the vehicle through which you experience the world. Your body helps you move from home to school, laugh with friends and enjoy life. So, take care of it.

Emotional Potential: You have a wide range of emotions, like happiness, sadness, anger, guilt and more. All these emotions serve a purpose in your life. Sometimes, you might be told to be happy all the time, but it's okay to feel other emotions too. It's important to learn how to handle and

channelize your feelings so you can feel good about life.

Mental Potential: Your mind is like a bridge between the past and the future. You learn from the past and imagine things for the future. Balancing your thoughts and using your mind wisely is important for your well-being.

Personal Potential: Do you feel worthy and love yourself? Just like looking after a little baby, you need to take care of yourself too. Celebrate who you are and how you feel about your life.

Social Potential: It's important to have basic social skills like greeting people, smiling and listening. It's not about making friends with everyone but about getting along with people in a respectful way.

Choices: Your choices are like a passport to freedom. They determine how you experience life. So, making good choices is crucial to keeping anxiety at bay.

By nurturing each of these segments of the whole person model wheel, you have the power to manage anxiety and live a balanced, joyful life.

REMINDER:

You are doing really

really well. Keep going,

and hang in there!

YOU GOT THIS!

Section 5

Understanding Anxiety in Specific Situations

CHAPTER 1

Anxiety Due to Learning Difficulties

Do you ever feel like learning is tricky? For some kids, it can be trickier because they have something called Learning Difficulties (LDs). Sometimes, along with LDs, they also have another sneaky thing called anxiety. It's like having two puzzles to solve at the same time.

Learning Difficulties (LD) are like roadblocks in the brain. They make it harder for some kids to learn and use certain skills, like reading, writing, listening, talking, thinking and solving problems. But not everyone with LD has the same problems. Some may find reading and writing tricky, while others might struggle with numbers.

1. Learning stuff feels like lifting heavy weights.

2. Reading, writing or solving problems might feel like climbing a mountain.

3. Sometimes, it's hard to stay interested or excited about learning.

4. You might feel frustrated or annoyed when things get tough.

5. You might not feel as good as your friends in class.

6. You might feel tired easily because the brain is working extra hard.

Anxiety:

The thoughts in your brain are like scary monsters, always making you scared or worried. You're scared of not doing things perfectly, like tests or homework. You feel nervous, your hands get sweaty and your heart beats fast. Sometimes, you avoid starting things because you fear that they might not be perfect. You feel shy or afraid to try new things because of worrying. Sometimes, LD and anxiety can all be friends and hang out together.

LD and Anxiety:

Sometimes, it's like having a super jumpy body because of all the worries.

The brain gets so busy worrying that it forgets to pay attention.

Finishing schoolwork feels like climbing a mountain because the brain is too busy worrying or not understanding.

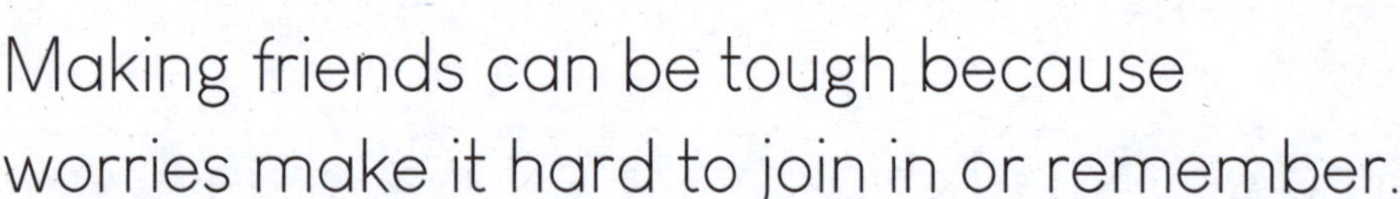

Making friends can be tough because worries make it hard to join in or remember.

Research shows that kids with LD and anxiety might face some extra challenges. They might not feel as good as others or struggle to finish things on time. Did you know that around 2% of people face challenges when it comes to learning? They might find some things a bit harder than others, and that's okay!

Imagine you're one of these people. You're in school, trying your best, but sometimes, reading or understanding things just doesn't come as easily. It's tough, especially when you're asked to read aloud in front of everyone else. Even if the teacher is nice, the fear can still be there.

Then, someone tells you that you have something called dyslexia, which is a word for brain difference that makes reading a bit harder. At first, it might feel like a relief to know there's a reason for the struggle. But sometimes, it can also make you feel like reading isn't worth the effort.

Let us understand this with the help of Siya.

Siya was a bright kid in grade 4, but she always felt like something was holding her back. She struggled with reading and writing, often mixing up letters and feeling lost in class. Despite her efforts, she couldn't seem to keep up with her classmates.

As the days went by, Siya's worries grew bigger. She felt like she was falling behind, and the fear of being seen as a failure weighed heavily on her. One day, during a class activity, she filled out a worksheet backwards, and that small mistake triggered her first panic attack.

Feeling overwhelmed and alone, Siya started to withdraw from her classmates. She stopped speaking in class and spent recess sitting by herself on a bench, trying to make sense of her thoughts. She knew something was wrong, but she didn't know how to fix it.

Thankfully, Siya's parents noticed her struggles and took her to a specialist. After a series of tests, Siya was diagnosed with dyslexia, dysgraphia and an auditory processing delay. It was a relief to finally have answers, but the fear of being judged never fully went away.

Siya's parents decided to enroll her in a school that specialized in helping kids with learning differences. With the support of her teachers and classmates, Siya started to make progress. She learned new strategies to help her read and write, and slowly but surely, her confidence began to grow.

However, despite her improvements, Siya still battled with anxiety. The fear of failure loomed over her, and she often felt like she was running away from a monster inside her own mind. She didn't want to admit that she needed help, fearing the stigma that came with it.

It wasn't until Siya's junior year of college that she finally reached her breaking point. Her anxiety had become overwhelming, affecting her grades and her daily life. With tears in her eyes, she finally sought help from a therapist.

Through therapy and medication, Siya learned to manage her anxiety. She no longer believed the lies her mind told her and she hadn't had a panic attack in over a year. But looking back, she wished she had sought help sooner.

Siya's story is not unique. Many kids struggle with learning difficulties and anxiety, but with the right support and understanding, they can thrive. Siya's journey taught her the importance of asking for help and speaking up about her struggles. And she hopes that by sharing her story, she can help others feel less alone in their own battles.

So, instead of putting labels on kids who learn differently, let's create spaces where everyone can learn and grow in their own special way. Because when we do, amazing things can happen!

CHAPTER 2

Anxiety Due to Menarche

Puberty is like a magical time when our body goes through a lot of big changes, and one of those changes for girls is something called menstruation. It's when a girl's body gets ready for the possibility of having a baby someday. This process starts with something called a period.

But for many girls, period can bring along extra challenges, especially when it comes to feelings. You see, when girls start having their periods, it can sometimes make them feel a bit anxious or stressed. This can happen because of a lot of different reasons, like feeling a bit scared about what's happening to their bodies.

Doctors say that these feelings can even affect how our bodies work! When we're feeling stressed, our bodies release special chemicals that can sometimes mess up our menstrual cycle, like delaying it or making it irregular.

Scientists are still learning about how emotions, periods and moods are linked. But here's what they know: Some girls might experience changes in the mood before or during their periods. This can happen because of something called premenstrual syndrome (PMS). PMS can make girls feel moody, cranky and tired, just like how they might feel when they're sad or anxious. These feelings can get stronger at certain times during their periods, which can make it harder to understand and manage their emotions. Hormonal changes during periods can also affect how our brains work and lead to shifts in emotions.

It's important to know that we're not alone in feeling this way. Lots of girls go through the same thing, and there are ways to feel better.

Managing Anxiety and Menstruation

1. Seek Support: Talking to someone you trust, like a parent, friend or healthcare professional, can provide emotional support and guidance.

2. Practice Self-Care:
Incorporate relaxation techniques, such as deep breathing exercises, meditation or yoga into your daily routine to reduce stress and promote emotional well-being.

3. Maintain a Balanced Lifestyle:
Prioritize regular physical activity, as exercise has been shown to reduce symptoms of anxiety and depression by releasing feel-good hormones called endorphins.

4. Educate Yourself: Learn more about anxiety, depression and menstruation to better understand your experiences and identify coping strategies that work for you.

5. Practice Mindfulness:
Incorporate mindfulness practices into your daily life, such as mindful breathing, body scans or mindful eating, to cultivate present-moment awareness and reduce rumination.

6. Establish Healthy Coping Mechanisms: Identify healthy coping mechanisms to manage stress and regulate your emotions, such as journaling, drawing or spending time in nature.

7. Stay Connected: Maintain meaningful connections with friends, family and supportive peers who uplift and validate your experiences.

8. Prioritize Self-Compassion: Be gentle with yourself and practice self-compassion, recognizing that it's okay to struggle and that you're deserving of kindness and understanding.

Let's walk through this "period" with the story of Tia.

Tia was a cheerful and curious girl who loved playing with her friends and exploring the world around her. One sunny afternoon, Tia's mom called her into the living room for a special talk. Tia's heart raced with excitement and a hint of nervousness as she wondered what her mom wanted to discuss.

Sitting down beside her mom, Tia listened intently as her mom explained something important: periods. Her mom spoke gently, using simple words to explain how every girl's body goes through changes as they grow up, and periods were a part of that journey.

Tia felt a mixture of emotions swirling inside her. She was curious to learn about this new thing her mom was talking about, but she also felt a little anxious. What if it was scary or painful?

As the days passed, Tia couldn't shake the feeling of butterflies in her stomach. She found herself thinking more and more about what her mom had told her. Would she be ready when the time came? What if she didn't know what to do?

One morning, Tia woke up feeling different. She felt a strange sensation in her tummy, like something was about to happen. When she went to the bathroom, she discovered a tiny spot of blood in her underwear. At first, Tia's heart skipped a beat. Then she remembered her mom's words about periods and realized that this was it–she was getting her first period!

Mixed with excitement and a bit of nervousness, Tia ran to tell her mom, Tia shared the news. Her mom smiled warmly and hugged her tight, reassuring her that everything was okay. Tia's dad joined in, offering words of encouragement and support. Feeling relieved and supported, Tia faced her first period with courage. Her friends also came to her aid, sharing their own stories and offering helpful tips. With each passing day, Tia felt more confident and comfortable with this new chapter of her life.

CHAPTER 3

Anxiety Due to Puberty

Ever wondered why your voice is cracking or why your hair is growing in new places? That's your body changing! This amazing process is called puberty in boys.

Your Body's Map:

Imagine you're on a secret mission. Everyone has their own special map to guide them through this adventure called puberty. This map shows the cool changes happening to your body, like growing taller, getting stronger muscles and even growing hair in new places!

Doctors can help you understand your body's journey by using special tools like checkups or questionnaires. It's like having a guide on your journey!

Comparing Adventures:

Everyone's journey through puberty happens at their own pace. Some friends might start noticing changes earlier, while others might take a bit longer. It's like comparing different paths on a map—they all lead to the same place, but some are shorter or longer.

Feeling Different Is Okay:

Sometimes, you might feel different from your friends because you're changing at different speeds. That's totally okay! Remember, everyone has their own unique map and adventure.

If you ever have questions or feel confused about your changes, don't hesitate to talk to a grown-up you trust, like a parent, doctor or counselor. They can be your superhero guide, helping you answer your questions and feel confident on your amazing journey!

Why Puberty Can Be Anxiety-Provoking

Puberty is a time of incredible change, both physically and emotionally. While it's a natural and important part of growing up, it's also understandable why it can be stressful and anxiety-provoking for many young people. Here's a breakdown of some factors contributing to this anxiety:

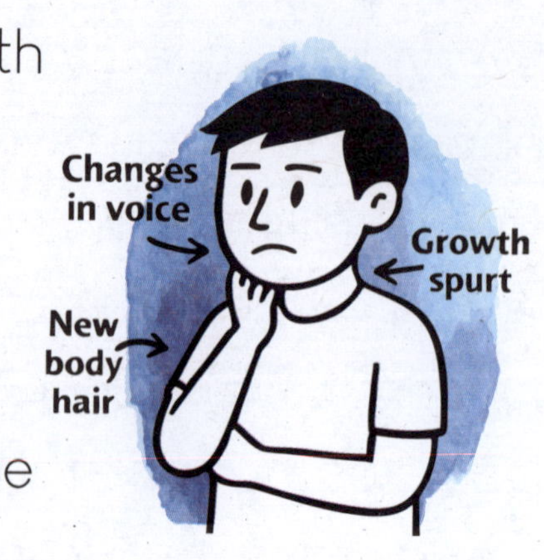

Rapid Physical Changes: Our bodies are going through a major transformation during puberty. We might experience growth spurts, new body hair and changes in our voices.

Social Pressures and Comparisons: As we develop, societal expectations and comparisons with peers can become more prominent.

Emotional Fluctuations: Hormonal shifts during puberty can also affect our emotions, making us feel more sensitive, irritable or unpredictable.